If Network Marketing is a Game These Are the Rules

Robert & Sheri Blackman

ISBN-13:
978-1983572401

ISBN-10:
1983572403

DEDICATION

We dedicate this book to every aspiring man or woman who is looking for the facts of what it really takes to build and maintain a Network Marketing organization.

CONTENTS

TESTIMONIALS

"Sheri Blackman is one of the most passionate women in the Network Marketing industry and is a true mentor and leader to women looking to blaze a new career path. The knowledge and direction that she and Robert bring to those who are just starting their careers is immeasurable. In a marketing world that is full of an immense amount of "noise", their step by step approach to success brings everything back down to the basics; providing rookies and veterans alike with a realistic and achievable method to building their organizations. I have personally known Robert and Sheri for close to 20 years. After finally stepping into a network marketing career myself, I look to them as mentors who beautifully light the way with proven successful actions and methods that I trust to take my business beyond levels that I could have ever dreamed! I am grateful to have been gifted with their friendship and leadership."

Erika Buzzard Wright
Wife, Mom, Business Owner, Successful Network Marketer

"This book came to me at a time when I was stuck. My up line was flourishing while my personal journey and downline was floundering. Network marketing is a journey, one that has highs and lows just like any career or business you will personally own. My background is in advertising and marketing so that part came easy for me, it was the relationships and working with my warm contacts that kept me growing. Getting back to the basics is what this book is all about, not only does it simplify but it frames a foundation providing a platform to continue to grow from. I have witnessed for over twenty years the dedication and tenacity Sheri and Robert have for direct sales and I can tell you there are no two people more determined for success. Their commitment to succeeding and ability to power through the down times is unprecedented."

Libby Blevins
Mom, Businesswoman, Successful Network Marketer

"I have been in and around the Network Marketing profession for 40+ years! When I met Robert I was immediately attracted to him because of his straightforward, no BS, "real world" business knowledge and deep personal philosophy!
He is an amazing cook and a ton of fun and his stuff is some of the best! So... if you're looking for "the real deal" or your thinking of creating some extra cash... or maybe even a fortune... let Robert and Sheri help you, they are "professionals", and make this book a "must read!"

Jay Coburn
Million Dollar Earner

"Within a few minutes of reading Robert & Sheri' new book, "If Network Marketing is a GAME These are the Rules" you will be clear that it comes from years of real life, no BS network marketing experience. The chapters on contacting are priceless! Robert & Sheri cover all bases and leaves nothing to chance. You will be a better Network Marketer after reading this book!"

Jordan Adler
Network Marketing Millionaire
Author of the Amazon Best Seller, "Beach Money" and "Better Than Beach Money"

"Robert and Sheri Blackman are a true power couple in the Network Marketing industry. I have known and been friends with Robert for more than a decade (Sheri and I have been friends since High School) and over the years have been amazed with 3 things in particular. First is their knowledge of the Network Marking industry. You would be hard pressed to find ANYONE that has their "finger on the pulse" more than the Blackmans. Second is there willingness to share this amazing amount of knowledge with anyone and everyone who wants to learn. They genuinely want you to succeed whether they financially benefit or not. I believe this is what makes them some of the top coaches and leaders in all of Network Marketing today.

The third thing that is amazing about this MLM power couple is their willingness to tell you about the tough times as well as the good. So often today people want to tell only part of a story, the part that makes them look good, but we all know this is not how the world works. The Blackmans willingness to be honest and set realistic and reasonable expectations is what makes them so unique and refreshing in this awesome industry!! This book is a compilation of decades of trial and error, what works and what doesn't, and simply reading the pages carefully can be life changing. As someone who has hit that magic six-figure a year mark in this industry I can tell you, having someone's years of experience to lean on makes all the difference. Thank you Robert and Sheri for giving so much of yourselves to help us all be better!!!"

Steve Bratcher, Six-Figure Income Earner

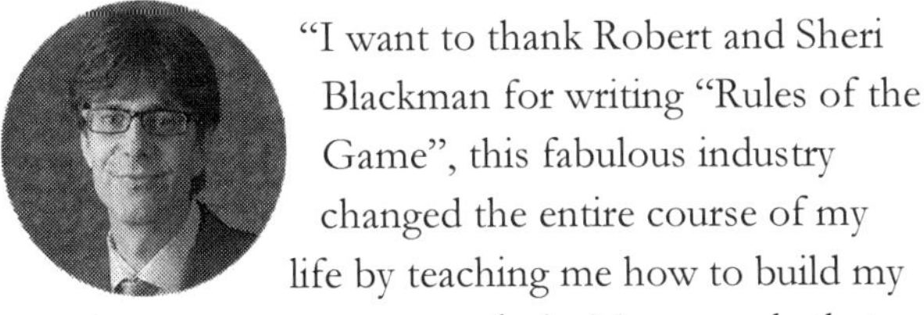

"I want to thank Robert and Sheri Blackman for writing "Rules of the Game", this fabulous industry changed the entire course of my life by teaching me how to build my own dreams verse someone else's. Most people that are financially free are in partnerships, if you are lucky enough to be Partners with Robert and Sheri they will teach you the Rules of the Game , however, if you are not lucky enough to be partners with them it is ok, they have put it all in this book. I can tell you there are few people that truly know how to build wealth more than Robert and Sheri, they do it with love and commitment, I am excited that everyone can be Partners now with them. Enjoy "Rules of the Game" folks and stop living everyone else's dreams. Live Yours!"

John Constatine, Co-Founder of Five Direct Sales, Insurance and Healthcare Companies

INTRODUCTION

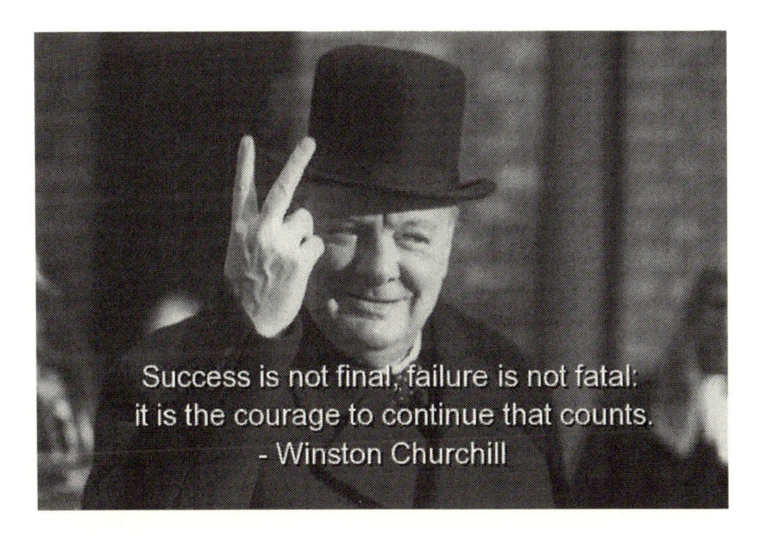

The purpose of this book is to help you build your Network Marketing business. The information, ideas, scripts and examples are from our combined 56 years of Network Marketing experience.

Feel free to share this with your downline and adapt any and all of it to your own personality. Throughout our Network Marketing Career, we have found some common "truths" that we will be sharing in this book.

Truths like:

- Network Marketing loves speed. That's why we are having you set a goal of reaching a certain Pin Level in your first (or your next) 90 days even though that might seem impossible to you at first. Slow and steady isn't the best way to create momentum. Build in 90-Day Spurts!

- The key to prospecting is creating and maintaining curiosity. The key to our methods is to get your prospects in your "Network Marketing Pipeline" to either become a customer or a distributor.

- Building a team is about duplication and finding and creating leaders. It's not about innovation. Although there are many ways to find customers and distributors the key for you to remember is *"can my team duplicate my methods?"* Within we focus on People You Know (family and friends) and People You Don't Know (telephone interviewed leads).

- *"Be the Messenger, not the Message"*. Point to the answers for your prospects and your team members. Don't make everything go through YOU. If you do, then you will become exhausted and burned out. Your team won't be able to do anything until they talk with you. Being the Messenger means knowing where to send people to get the information they need. Then following up to insure their questions are answered and signing them up as a customer, a distributor, or get referrals.

- Most people are afraid to contact their family and friends. And, for those that do contact them, they do it only once and that attempt is usually done with very little success. In Rule #2 we show you exactly how to tap into this valuable asset you possess.

- Investing in Telephone Interviewed leads. Most who have attempted this method have failed miserably. Not us.

- We have perfected this method by having a telephone center call the leads first and interview them. This dramatically increases your response and cuts down your time calling tire kickers. In Rule #3 we go into great detail on how to use this method effectively and how you can build your entire business around Telephone Interviewed Leads. Since most of our team members either refuse or won't contact those people they already know, this method is the purest form of duplication. Getting hot, qualified prospects in their hands every month on a consistent basis…thus, they never run out of people to talk to!

- You don't need any previous sales or business experience to succeed in Network Marketing. In fact, some who have the highest degrees in school and have achieved the highest levels in business find this business model difficult. Why? Because to achieve the highest levels in this profession you must learn to help others before you help yourself. You must learn to help them achieve their goals before you reach yours. Your focus should be on them, not you. You'll never see some of the greatest income earners in Network Marketing on social media or in the news because they have quietly and efficiently helped hundreds and thousands of others achieve their freedom. Thus, they become free in the process.

- When you think of contacting people about your program, think of the flu. It's your job to infect them with the "Network Marketing Flu". Some will be immune to this business model and even your products or services. That's okay. Expect it. Just know that we both have been infected with the Network Marketing Flu for a combined 56 years and we've found it to be the best ailment we've ever had!

Robert Says:

I have to admit that I am guilty of thinking that success in Network Marketing would be final with the first company I joined. I was wrong. I, like many others, encountered resistance and failure with my first few companies I joined. Just like dating, I didn't marry the first girl I went out with. Once I matured and understood this concept and focused on learning the fundamentals that I could apply to any company I joined, I excelled beyond my wildest dreams. If you are new to this profession know that you may not make it to the top in your first venture. That's okay, that's normal. If you have been in before and failed, go ahead and give it another try. This time armed with the proper techniques outlined here. If you are currently in the profession, bravo! Take these tips and watch your organization explode!

Sheri Says:

One of my all-time favorite quotes, success is not final. It's not a destination. And neither is failure, not while you still have breath. You can lose success just as you can lose failure. Continuous effort will move you through failure and on to success. Robert and I have seen our fair share of both. We thought success was a destination, and once you reached it, you could sit back and relax. Easy street. Ha! Nothing lasts if you stop it. Just like a light. When you turn off the electricity, that energy, the light goes off. If you turn off your energy, your effort, you'll stop too. Let these 7 Rules guide you along your path of growth in Network Marketing. The more knowledge you obtain, the more confident you will be, and the more energy you will have to launch your business. Now let's get started!

ROBERT'S STORY

I grew up in an oil town where the largest employer was a Top 100 company. My Father owned a printing manufacturing plant that ran 24 hours a day and 7 days a week.

My Mother owned her own beauty salon called "LaFemme". Both of my parents where hard working entrepreneurs in a corporate town.

The one event that changed my life was at age 16, my best friend and I were playing catch with a football in his front yard when his Dad suddenly drove up into their driveway.

I was the Quarterback and he was my center. In baseball I was the pitcher and he was my catcher. And, we both had the same birthday to boot…so we were best of friends.

This was odd, as it was a Monday morning and he was slumped over the steering wheel and he looked like he was sobbing. Before we got a chance to go over to the car, he got out and was carrying a small brown box.

He went to the front door where his wife met him, and she started crying.

He had been laid off after 35 years of loyal and dedicated service to just one company.

When he went to work that early Monday morning, he was met at the front door by two security officers and asked for his badge and keys. He was then handed a box of his personal affects that they had gathered the night before and handed it to him.

When he asked if he could go inside to at least say goodbye to his friends he was told a firm NO!

Thirty-five years of service, to only be met at the door and be treated like a vagabond!

That left a huge impact on me. This man had been my baseball coach since Little League. He was like a second Father to me. I vowed that day to never put my financial future in the hands of some corporation whose only interest was in the bottom line!

I had no idea what Network Marketing was at the time, I only knew I wanted to be my own boss and call my own shots, even if that meant making less money and working more hours. I wanted to be in control of my own financial destiny. My entire outlook on College and my career path changed that day.

SHERI'S STORY

With a Mom from Oklahoma and Dad from Texas, I grew up running up and down I-35 and I-45. Mom was an art teacher and Dad was the dreamer. The entrepreneur. Always thinking of different ways to make money.

He had been in the navy, worked as a cop, and at the sheriff's department as a jailer. But he always had big dreams. He loved to travel, so he became an over the road driver. Truck driving is a long hard job, and he was often gone.

But we made many trips with him all over the U.S.

He was the first system bucker I ever met. It had to be his way.

Compromises were made, sometimes. But most of the time he was Frank Sinatra, doing it his way. I was intrigued with his no nonsense, go get 'em approach.

Mom was the stable one and Dad was the feather. Teaching school meant Mom was usually home when we were. But she had an underlying current of entrepreneurship as well.

She became a distributor for a cosmetic company when I was in high school, and later a transfer buy company. She was always willing to give network marketing a try.

I didn't understand all of this at the time. I was too busy with sports and school. But these little glimpses I would catch of my parents trying to find a different way, a better way, stuck. Stuck in my psyche.

I wouldn't realize it until after college that I, too, was a square peg trying to fit into a round hole. I was not an 8-5 girl. I always felt like a caged bird. Looking for the opening so I could fly!

I wouldn't understand how all the pieces fit together until I met a man my senior year in college.

I was working as a waitress in a Mexican restaurant and he showed me some circles on a napkin.

"Yeah, yeah", I told him. *"It sure sounds good and all, but I'll try my hand out there in the real world and I'll let you know how it goes"*.

And the rest as they say, is history.

ACKNOWLEDGMENTS

There are many people who have had a positive impact on our careers.

Specifically, Dale Calvert, who taught us Rule #2.

And, Eric Worre whose training video taught us Rule #6.

John Merris who taught us what duplication really is and that if you build people, they will build the business. He also taught us to draw circles on a white board. His famous quote was: *"The person holding the marker is the person making the money"*.

Phil Longanecker who showed us the lead generation ropes.

And, to every speaker on stage we ever listened to. We learned to take at least one thing from all of your speeches and apply it to our business!

RULE #1 – THE HOW TO DOESN'T MATTER UNTIL YOU KNOW YOUR REASON'S WHY

Of all our 7 Rules this is by far the most important one. So, please don't skip it. Stop after reading this Rule and print out your "reasons why" sheet and get your entire organization to do the same.

We have found that this is the GLUE that holds our Network of independent reps all over the world together.

Why? Because Network Marketing consists mostly of part-time participants. Your entire sales organization is a volunteer army. That means you'll have to put a system in place that helps you identify the leaders from the tire-kickers and from the people who just want to be wholesale customers.

Most of your team will be currently employed with a 8-5 job. They work all day and give their best to building someone else's dream. Then, when they get home, instead of putting on their pj's, ordering a pizza and watching movies all night, you expect them to build a business with you instead.

Over 95% of those that you recruit on your team will have:

- No previous sales or business experience.
- No previous Network Marketing experience.
- No knowledge of how to contact anyone about your product or service and how to show them a presentation.
- Little or no self-esteem to talk to everyone they know, let alone strangers.
- Not a clue on how the compensation plan in your company works, nor how to get enough customers or reps to at least break-even, not to mention a proven formula to replace their income at work in the next 2-5 years!

Here's a chart from the DSA.org that explains this:

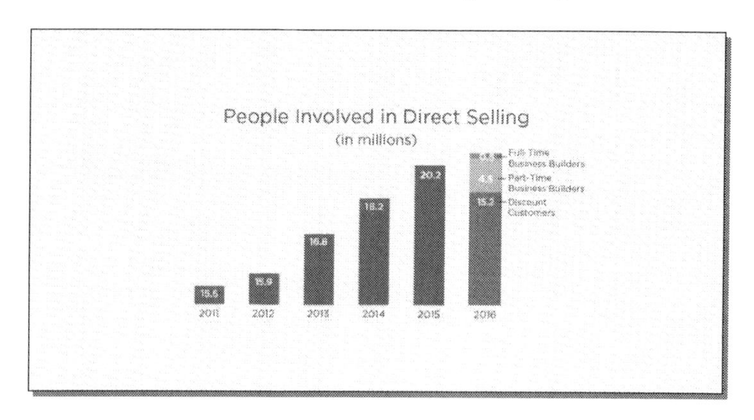

Very few people go full-time their first year in the business.

Most franchises cost a minimum of $100,000 to start and upwards of over a million dollars. Most Network Marketing companies cost anywhere from $100 to $1,000 to join.

That's a huge difference in investment and the mindset going into your business.

Just because it costs just a few hundred dollars to start, most distributors don't treat it like a $100,000 investment.

Before you learn the "How-To" in Network Marketing you need to take some time and define your "Top 3 Reasons Why" you got involved in the first place.

By doing so, you will not only gain clarity to why you joined this Profession, but you'll solidify your intent when times get tough and things don't seem to be going the way you thought they would.

If you have 100 people on your team and all 100 of them have their own list of "3 Reasons Why" next to their desk, your likelihood of success will be much higher than if you have just 10.

When we are sponsoring new people into our business, the very first thing we do is have them fill out their "3 Reasons Why".

If they don't, we know that the likelihood of them quitting in the next 90 days greatly increases.

Your goal is to get a game plan that allows you to replace your income at your job or business in the next 2-5 years. To do that, you'll need the efforts of others to get there.

That's called team building.

You can't just recruit or sell your way to replacing your income at work…that's nothing more than a glorified 100% commission job.

Instead, you want to learn how to tap into the real power of Network Marketing, which is:

DUPLICATION

We knew nothing about Network Marketing, nor what duplication even meant. In fact, when we started working together we both had jobs that paid us around $40,000 a year.

In the next few years we saw our income grow to over $40,000 a month with these 7 simple rules! Here's a snapshot of our "Top 3 Reasons Why" sheet we carry with us:

Robert's Top Three Reasons Why:

1. Be My Own Boss
2. Be Debt Free – Pay All Bills In Advance On 1st
3. Live to Age 100 Healthy

Sheri's Top Three Reasons Why:

1. More Time With My Family
2. Be Debt Free
3. Travel the World

Print one out for you and print one out for your spouse, or significant other.

If you have a boyfriend or a girlfriend, get them to fill one out with you, or at least tell them why you're doing this…to make a difference in your life and possibly theirs!

Letting your family and friends know what you are doing is a very significant thing. If nobody in your sphere of influence supports you, don't worry, you're not alone, that's not uncommon. Stop right now and fill out your top three reasons why on the next page. Have your spouse or partner do the same:

My Top Three Reasons Why:

1. ______________________________________

2. ______________________________________

3. ______________________________________

My Top Three Reasons Why:

1. ______________________________________

2. ______________________________________

3. ______________________________________

My Top Three Reasons Why:

1. ______________________________________

2. ______________________________________

3. ______________________________________

IMPORTANT POINT: DO get a copy of your "Top Three Reasons Why" into the hands of your sponsor or upline that you are working with so they know your Reasons Why!

And, more importantly, have everyone on your team get their copy to you as well.

Also, put a copy of your "Top Three Reasons Why":

- In your wallet
- In your purse
- On the door on the way out to your garage
- On the door on the way into your house
- Your bedroom door
- Your bathroom door
- Your bathroom mirror
- The door into your closet
- Next to your computer at home
- Next to your computer at work (if allowed)
- On the refrigerator
- In the car
- In the pantry
- Guys, next to the grill outside (yes, laminate them)
- Guys, on the back of the remote control!
- Gals, use it as a book marker
- And, most importantly, next to your phone!

You get the idea!

Place your "Top Three Reason's Why" everywhere as a constant reminder why you're building your business.

Is it for your retirement? Replace your income at work? To get out of credit card debt? Get a new car that starts every time you turn the key? Get a bigger house? The kid's college education? Pay off back taxes? Help a loved one?

Join the gym? Hire a personal trainer? Get a nanny? Have a weekly date night (remember those?) Give more to your favorite charity or church? Whatever your REASONS are, write them down and put them where you will see them on a daily basis to help you FOCUS on your business!

Robert Says:

When I first started in Network Marketing I was making $10 an hour running a printing press for my Father. I took home before taxes $1600 a month. So, I had a $1600 a month dream. I kept thinking how great my life would be to never have to go to that plant again…if I just worked hard enough I could replace my income at work and be home all day and night. I could do what I wanted to do, when I wanted to do it and with the people I wanted to do it with. I sat down with my sponsor and found out EXACTLY how much sales I needed, what pin level that was and how many people it would take. I put my head down and never looked back!

Sheri Says:

Network Marketing was such an enigma to me in the beginning. I knew it was a better way, I was just fearful of taking that first leap. But getting up at 5:30 am to get our son to daycare so I could work a 10-hour day and have a three-day weekend was taking its toll. Trading hours for dollars was no Bueno. Yeah, I had a three-day weekend, but Sunday was always a struggle. Ugh! Early to bed and early up to start it all again. Off to build someone else's dream while someone else raised my child. The why mommy! Don't leave! Nope. Right there. Big reason #1. I made the decision. No leap, it was a head first dive!!

RULE #2: CONTACTING PEOPLE YOU KNOW

Normally in Network Marketing you are asked to make a list of 100 names and either you or you and your sponsor get on the phone and call them and invite them to a meeting.

If you have no upline support, what normally happens is, you sit down to make that list and you don't come up with 100.

You come up with about 17 people. You call the first 5 and you get 4 voice mails and 1 person says no. You hang up the phone and vow to never call another person again.

Sound familiar?

It should. It's the number one reason why calling your family and friends has such a bad stigma around it.

Because we have a print and direct mail background. We decided, years ago, to do something different than our upline.

We decided to act like we owned a yogurt shop instead of a Network Marketing business.

We decided to mail our family and friends EVERY MONTH.

Before we go into the "how-to" here's a quick outline of how the program works.

1. Make a list of at least 100 people you already know. Get their mailing addresses as well. If you don't have their mailing address text, call or email them for it.

2. Customize the letter in this chapter with your information on it. Mail 25 letters on every Friday for the next four weeks. Why Friday? Because when you mail on Friday they will receive your letter on Monday, Tuesday or Wednesday. That allows you to make follow up calls the next week.

3. So, the routine is to mail 25 letters on Friday, make follow up phone calls to see if they got your letter on Monday thru Wednesday. If they live in the same town, call those people on Monday. If they live across the country call them on Wednesday.

4. At the end of four weeks you will have mailed and called 100 people! The majority of the people who follow this method will sign up 5-10 customers and/or distributors over a 90-day period. You'll notice in the scripts below we are asking for a referral first…this is the way you can take this list of 100 and turn it into a list of 200, 300 or more! Get your team to duplicate this in their first (or next) 30 days and you'll see an explosion in your business!

5. You must realize when calling your family and friends the odds that the person you are talking to about your

Network Marketing business being the person you are looking for are very low. But, the chances they know someone who you are looking for is very high.

Now let's teach you the how to…

Most distributors make the mistake of trying to convince everyone they know to join with them. Sometimes they even pay for their membership and products, which never works long term.

Look, a person's window is either open or it's not.

You are not looking to force people's windows open.

Instead, when they open the window, you want to be the one standing outside ready to give them a helping hand.

You are looking for people who are looking for you! You're looking for people who are sick and tired of being sick and tired. You're looking for people who are ready to do something different with their lives and they are no longer satisfied with the "status quo" or the 9 to 5 routine.

- You're looking for employees who are tired of building their boss's dream.
- You are looking for traditional small business owners who are tired of their businesses running them into the ground 24/7.
- And, you're looking for people who want to improve their lives with your products or services that your Network Marketing company offers.

You're looking for people who are tired of being broke. Tired of having a dream of doing more with their life, but they don't know what to do and who to turn to!

You're not looking to convince anyone of the benefits of being a distributor with you just so you can make money.

Normally, when you contact your family and friends about this business and nobody joins, you get discouraged and quit.

You might be thinking: *"I contacted everyone I know about joining as a distributor and nobody joined, now what do I do?"*

The purpose of Rule #2 is to help you avoid this most common mistake in Network Marketing.

Tens of thousands of people join a Network Marketing company every week. There are over 10 million reps worldwide.

You are looking for people whose window is open. What do I mean by that? Something happened in their life that has opened their window.

And, when their window is open they are ready to listen to an alternative way of making money, which is Network Marketing.

They are ready to receive.

A large number of people's windows are not open now…but that doesn't mean it will never be open in the near future.

That is why the way you approach people when their window is closed is VERY important.

So, when you contact someone about your business the odds are very slim that their window is open at that moment in time.

Don't make the mistake of being a window breaker.

Your job isn't to open people's windows…your job is to be there when people open up their window, which is a huge difference. And, this is the #1 reason why most distributors get discouraged and quit with this method.

They can't understand why someone won't join when they barge into their life by smashing open their window.

In 365 days out of the year, we believe that everyone's window opens up at least once for your product/service/opportunity!

What are some things that make people's window open?

- They didn't get that promotion they were counting on
- Their car needs repairs they can't afford
- Maybe their mortgage payment just went up
- Maybe their company is laying off good people
- An illness in their family caused a financial stress

Amateurs in this business try to convince people when they first contact them. Professionals, on the other hand, learn to sort through people and ask for referrals.

It's a whole lot easier working with people who have their own reasons for doing this business, rather than them just saying yes so you won't bother them anymore. See the difference?

That's why getting your own "Top 3 Reasons Why" is so important. That's why you need to get your downlines "Top 3 Reasons Why".

If you have a team of 20 distributors and none of them will fill out a card of their top 3 reasons why and give it to you, what does that tell you about your organization?

Is it more likely to grow quickly or is it more likely to fade quickly?

Likewise, take those same 20 people, and if 5 of them get their top 3 reasons back to you, what do you think is about to happen to your business?

It's about to grow!

Get those 3 reasons why quickly! Those are the people you will want to work with now!

Get them to make their top 100 prospects over the next four weeks (mail 25 letters a week and call 25 a week per the training in this manual).

That's how you get your current group to grow. And that's how you get your check to grow even if you don't personally sponsor someone this month.

This business is about finding and developing leadership.

It's not about being a Network Marketing salesperson.

Yes, you want to sponsor new customers and new distributors every month. But, not at the expense of finding and developing leaders.

If you spend all your time bringing in 100 new customers and distributors a month how are you ever going to find time to teach and train them?

The answer is you won't.

And the conclusion of that process is you'll simply be replacing those that you sponsored three months ago with new signups you put in this month.

It becomes a revolving door and your business eventually hits a wall. Your check stops at a certain level and then drops back 10% to 25% and you never seem to regain any momentum.

That happens when duplication stops.

Duplication occurs when everyone is on the same page.

They are getting their three reasons to their sponsor and they are contacting their top 100 prospects by mailing (or calling) at least 25 letters a week.

Plus, with the next Rule, we'll show you how to get an endless supply of hot prospects to talk to from our Phone Room. This will help your business explode!

Remember, people do things for their own reasons, not yours. What's important to you may or may not be important to them.

Some people may be very happy with their job and their income level. But, they will join your program anyway just because of the products or service you provide, as a retail customer or wholesale distributor.

Find out what motivates your downline and work with them to achieve their goals, not yours, and you'll start to see your downline grow!

Now, before we go into what to say and what to get in your prospects hands, I want you to understand this concept:

"You could have a lousy website/CD/DVD/video, stutter when you talk and even not remember the name of your company when you talk to someone. But, if their window is open they'll take a close look at what you are doing by asking you for more information. And, you could have the best CD/DVD/video ever made on the planet and the #1 rated website in the country, and if their window isn't open, nothing you can say or do will make them join. You can't say anything wrong to the right person and you can't say anything right to the wrong person! It's their open window you are looking for…you and I already know our window is open 365 days a year, but most of the people who you talk to have a closed window. So, don't get discouraged when you run into a closed window. Approach them in a professional way so when their window does open they remember you!"

The name of the Network Marketing game is sorting and sifting, looking for open windows! The only thing you can control is the number of people you and your organization contact on a monthly, weekly and daily basis.

Have you ever contacted someone about your business and they said no only to find out a few months later they joined another program?

What happened?

Their window was open one day and someone else was standing there outside of their window instead of you.

Stop trying to tell people that "they'd be great at this business". Don't convince, sort!

Our system works because of this very simple 4-step process

1) Contact your list of 100+ prospects by phone, mail, email or text. We prefer mailing a letter as it has more of an impact than any other method we've used.

2) Invite them to watch a video and give you a referral. Try to get as many referrals as possible, but a minimum of three from each of your 100. That gives you 300 new people to contact, which gives you plenty of people to talk to!

3) Lead with a product or service vs. leading with the opportunity. But, use your own best judgment as you know your list better than anyone. If you know someone is business minded or has been in Network Marketing before or even now, lead with the opportunity.

4) If you have a list of 100 contacts mail 25 letters a week and the next week call 5 people a day to follow up.

Okay, here's how you get your business off the ground and in the right direction your first 30 days and beyond.

Get your list of warm market prospects and either mail them a letter, or pick up the phone and call them.

If you prefer to call your top 100 contacts, here is what you say to them on the phone, or in person:

"Hi John, this is (your name). How are you doing? Hey, I wanted to know if you can do me a favor and help me out? I just got involved in a new business and I'm really excited about it! I'm looking for a couple of key people with leadership and management abilities and I naturally thought of you. I have no idea John if you'd be personally interested, but I know you know the right kind of people that I'm looking for. What I need you to do is watch a short video and tell me who you know that I should contact. What email address should I send the link to?

Here are the reasons why this approach works when you are looking for distributors:

1. If someone you know is excited about something, human nature says you want to know what it is that has them so pumped up and motivated. They are curious and will be opened minded to find out what is exciting one of their friends.

2. You also just complimented them by *saying "I'm looking for a couple of key people with leadership and management abilities and I naturally thought of you".* You just stroked their ego and patted them on the back as well both at the same time!

3. Now, you're going to relieve any potential stress and tension by saying: *"I have no idea John if you'd be personally interested, but I know you know the right kind of people I'm looking for".* You can almost hear the sigh of relief on the other end of the phone, or if you are in person you can see the expression on their face show "relief" when you say that statement. You've given them an out, or what we call in sales a "takeaway" and you've postured yourself to the point of almost guaranteeing they'll give you some great referrals.

4. About 9 out of 10 people will say *"sure, I'll watch it for you and let you know who I can recommend".* You make it easy now for your 100 family and friends to tell you YES, rather than NO. Don't try to overcomplicate this process. It works because it's simple. It works because trying to convince your family and friends to join a Network Marketing program with you doesn't work…the data after almost 60 years shows that. So, use this approach and teach this to your downline so they can start seeing more "YES's" than "NO's" in their first 30-days of business with you!

Even if your best friend says:

"No thank you, I'm not interested." You go ahead and say: *"I didn't think you would be interested, but I still need your help. I need you to watch the video and tell me who you know who might be interested because I'm very excited about this and would really appreciate you doing me this favor!"*

Some people might say:

"I really don't know anybody".

You go ahead and say:

"John, I don't expect you to know anybody until you see the video. What email do you want me to send it to?"

Always try to deal with any objection by agreeing with them. Then, focus on getting your information in front of them.

- Agree.
- Get your video link to them.

Also, if they try to get you to tell them about it over the phone, don't. That never works. You only give them some ammunition for them to say everyone they know wouldn't be interested in that and you ruin your chance for getting them in or getting referrals from them.

If they do, try to get you to tell them more on the phone or in person go ahead and say:

"John, if I tried to do that it would take me over an hour and the video does it in a much shorter amount of time".

You've got to get the video in their hands so it can go to work for you. You're not trying to be evasive, you're just letting the tools do their job for you. Duplication occurs when everyone on your team is passing out videos and not saying very much on the phone or in person.

The less YOU say in this business the more money YOU make.

Recruiting is about creating and maintaining curiosity.

As soon as you say skin care, nutritional product, or weight loss, a red flag immediately goes up with your prospect and a pre-conceived notion (good or bad) then comes flying back at you with a *"I wouldn't be interested in that, and neither would anyone I know, but thanks anyway".*

You want ZERO preconceptions when they sit down and watch the video.

I know that might be against what you've been taught in the past, but the tools are a 3rd party endorsement of your program…let them do their job for you!

Your friends are much more likely to believe a person who they don't know on a video than you anyway.

Why? Because they are too close to you. They know too much about you. Let the tools do the talking for you and spend your time contacting more people!

Follow-up: (Call or mail 25 people a week for 4 weeks for a total of 100). Duplicate this for everyone you personally sponsor into your business. When done correctly you will never run out of prospects to contact!

Now that you've contacted your first 25 people, you and your sponsor can do a 3-way call together by saying the following: (or you can call yourself, but get help, if you need it):

> *"Hey John, this is (your name), I just wanted to follow up with you about the video I sent you. I have my business partner (your sponsors name) on the phone with me."*

Don't say another word…be quiet.

You are then waiting for your prospect to make the first move and whatever they say, you remain quiet and your sponsor then answers questions.

The reason why you remain quiet is if you say something your friends are not as likely to believe you as they would a stranger.

Your friends and relatives will be harsh with you on the phone, but they usually won't be harsh with a stranger…it's human nature.

Your sponsor then will say something along these lines:

> *"Hi John, this is (their name). We don't want to take a lot of your time tonight we are just calling to see if you've had a chance to watch the video."*

Your prospect is going to say one of three things:

- Yes, I've watched it
- Yes, I've watched it and I don't think I would be interested.
- No, I haven't watched it yet

That's the only three things they will say.

Here's how you respond to each one of those:

- **Yes, I've watched it:**

  Your sponsor says: *"Great, are you open for more information?"* If they say yes, then you want to take them to the next step which could be a local meeting, a one-on-one meeting at a coffee shop, a conference call or a website. To get them to your event you say: *"Great, what are you doing Monday night? What we would like to do is dial you into our conference call, our meeting, etc."* That's how you turn a yes into getting them to the next step. Make sure you say: *"What are you doing Monday night"* instead of: *"Great, I need to get you to a meeting or I need you get you on our next conference call."* If you do it that way, they'll always have a reason they can't make it. Ask them what they are doing first on the night of your event so the logical conclusion is if they aren't doing anything they can attend with you.

- **Yes, I've watched it and I don't think either I or anyone I know would be interested.**

  You sponsor says: *"No problem. Let me ask you a question. If you were going to do this business who'd be the first person you'd talk to?"* They might say Mary. Then you say: *"Why Mary?"* Get as much information as you can about Mary (phone, address, email, etc.) and contact Mary the same way. You then say: *"Who'd be the second person you'd talk to?" "Who else do you know that we should contact?"* Again, the odds of the person who you know being the one you are looking for are slim. But, the odds of them knowing someone who you are looking for are much higher.

Don't try to do what every other unsuccessful Network Marketers has done.

They call up all their friends and tell them they have to join with them in a new Network Marketing program. That doesn't work. There's a 99% chance their window is closed the day you call them. That's why we also recommend that you get all your family and friends and co-workers on your product or service to help them solve a problem. Let the product help you open up their window. It's easier to get a customer than a distributor—so get them on the product or service first if they resist becoming a distributor. By only contacting your list of 100 people one way and one way only, via getting them in the opportunity as a distributor you are severely limiting your exposure.

Get referrals! Get referrals!

➢ **No, I haven't watched it yet:**

Your sponsor is going to say: "*Hey, no problem. Do you have a pen? Great, here's my phone number. The video is very informative. Could you watch it tonight and just give me a call when you are finished?" I'm going to be up late and it doesn't matter what time it is.*" A lot of times people will say yes. Other times they will say they have other plans and they can't watch it tonight. Simply ask them when would be a good time for them to watch it, or do they know of anyone who would like to make an extra thousand or two a month? Then, your next step is to get your upline on the phone with the referral from one of your contacts that you have sent your video link to.

Your upline says this:

"Hi James, this is (your sponsors name), you don't know me, but we have a mutual friend in (your name). (Your name) and I are involved in a new business together and we are looking to expand into your area. I just wanted to let you know that we've got a short online video that I'd like to send you. What email can I send that to? And, when do you think you could watch it so I can follow up and find out who you think we should talk to about this program?"

- Fear of loss.
- Maintain curiosity
- Sense of urgency.

These are three key factors in getting those people on your list to make a decision.

Don't chase people. Don't beg them to watch the video or come to a meeting.

You move them to action in an excited and professional way!

NOTE: If you satisfied someone's curiosity there is no reason for them to come to your local meeting. There's no reason for them to get on your conference call. There's no reason to watch the video. There's no reason to meet with you at a coffee shop or come to your home meeting.

If you can't get people to a local meeting and you can't get people to a conference call, then you and your organization are telling the prospects too much information!

Don't be evasive. Just tell them that all their questions can be answered at the "meeting" or on the "video" and that you have other calls to make.

Again, the less you say the more money you make in Network Marketing.

The biggest fault of excited Networkers is that they want to tell everyone how excited they are about the product, the company, the pay plan, the online system.

Remember, what excites you about your program may not interest any of the 100 people who you first contact.

There are only three types of people you'll ever contact about your Network Marketing Program:

- Someone with no prior Network Marketing experience
- Someone who was in a program before but they aren't now
- Someone who is in one or more programs now

Each of these three types of people will be looking, listening, and gathering information differently. Let the TOOLS do the work for you.

Let the meeting, the video, the CD, the conference call, the brochure, or the website make the initial impression for you.

Then, answer their questions. And, if you're concerned they'll ask you a question you're not ready to answer yet, get your upline to help you.

Repeat this process to all of your prospects.
Repeat this process to all of your downlines prospects.

This is a proven duplicatable system.

Get help from your upline leader to implement this program.

I want you to understand that if you call and follow up with five people, one of them is probably going to have an interest in getting more information about the business. But, four of them won't be.

As soon as they say: *"No, I don't think this is for me."* They are expecting a hard sell from you. They are expecting someone to try and close them into the program.

But, when you get an objection and you say, *"no problem"*, it almost stops them in their tracks to where they wonder why you're not trying harder to get them to join.

(You mean you don't want me?)

Get a referral for your product/service/business.

Ask them who is the first person or second person they can think of who would be interested in your product, service or business opportunity.

We've even had people tell us: *"I'm not going to give you any of my good people!"*

And, we'll say: *"Well, I thought you weren't open for more information?"*

You'll be amazed at the number of people who put their guard up if they think you are trying to sell them something.

Just go into a department store and you get hit up by a salesperson who says: *"Hello, can I help you?"*

What's the most likely answer you'll give them? *"No, I'm just looking?"*

The same goes with this business. Nobody wants to be sold.

A lot of times people's natural reaction is to say that this business isn't for them, when they don't even know what the product is or what the business is!

Sample Phone Script Review:

"Hi John, this is (your name). How are you doing? Hey, I wanted to know if you can do me a favor and help me out? I just got involved in a new business and I'm really excited about it and I'm looking for a couple of key people with leadership and management abilities and I naturally thought of you. I have no idea John if you'd be personally interested, but I know you know the right kind of people that I'm looking for. What I need you to do is watch a short video online and tell me who you know who I should contact. What email address should I send the link to?

Now that you've learned the sample "Phone Script", on the following two pages are a sample letter you send in the mail.

There is also a sample text or inbox on social media to get your prospects physical address.

Plus, a sample postcard you can mail MONTHLY to your family and friends! (Mail the postcard on month two and beyond after you send this letter on month one).

Our system works because we do much, much more than just make a list of 100 names and call them.

It's inappropriate to call your family and friends every month.

But, it's normal to MAIL them a postcard about your company every month…just like every other traditional business in their home town does.

Here is a sample letter to mail:

Hi (Prospects Name),

The purpose of this letter is to let my friends, family and business associates know that I have started a new business and I'm very excited about it!

I am working with a company called XYZ out of City, State. Their products (or services) include:

- Product
- Product

I'm looking for people with leadership and management abilities and I naturally thought of you. I have no idea if you'd be interested or not, but I'm sure you know of someone who would be.

I need a favor; can you help me out?

Could you visit my website and watch this quick video and tell me who you know that I should talk to:

www.YourWebsiteGoesHere.com

I will call you in a couple of days to see who you think I should contact. Thanks in advance for your help, I really appreciate it.

Warmly,

Your Picture, Name and Phone Number

PS Thank you for your help, I am very excited about our new business and appreciate your referrals!

Sample text to People You Know:

Hi John, I need a quick favor? I'm updating all my contact lists and can you send me your physical address? Thanks!

Sample Postcard to Mail Monthly:

October Update from Robert & Sheri Blackman

- This Month's Product Special is: www.ProductSpecialLink.com
- 24-Hour Information Hotline: www.RecordedConferenceCall.com
- Call us at: (405) 833-6899 for more Info.

Please send anyone you know who is interested in starting their own "Amazon Type" business to this website now:

www.VisitOurWebsite.com

As you can see there is nothing fancy about this postcard.

We designed it in a Word document and print them out from our own ink jet printer each month.

The concept I want you to take away today is this:

"What if you owned a Yogurt shop in your home town? Wouldn't you contact your family and friends monthly to come down and buy from you?"

The answer is "YES", of course you would!

So, don't fall into the trap that you shouldn't or can't contact your family and friends more than once about your business.

YOU CAN and YOU SHOULD!

I can't tell you the number of referrals and people who have run us down in church parking lots, at the grocery store or even at one of our kid's ballgames who had one of these postcards in their hands!

Your family & friends want to know that you're going to stick with it.

And, by mailing them a postcard MONTHLY they see that you are going places.

Plus, this is a great way to showcase your entire product line!

Remember, It's Easier to Get a Customer Than Sign Up a Distributor in Network Marketing.

Why?

To become a distributor and start your own business your mind goes through this kind of checklist:

- How much is it going to cost?
- Which credit card am I going to put that on?
- I wonder when I'll break even?
- Who am I going to talk to?
- When am I going to find the time?
- I don't have any sales experience; how can I do this?
- What will my spouse, family or friends think?
- I don't want to let you down if I don't follow through.
- My wife/husband/parents are going tell me don't do it.

To become a customer your mind goes through this kind of checklist:

- I wonder how much it is going to cost?
- Can I get my money back if it doesn't work?
- If I don't like it, I just won't buy it again.
- My friend seems excited, I'll buy it to make them happy and help them succeed.

See the different thought process?

Sure, if your best friend is a super-duper sales person, go get them as a distributor.

But, if you owned a yogurt franchise you wouldn't be going to all your family and friends asking them to buy a franchise too, would you?

You wouldn't be saying:

"If I sell three franchises I can get my investment back, so I need you to sign up today for me to be successful!"

Our best distributors have come from happy customers.

Our best distributors have come from friends of ours who were customers first. They talked about our products to someone they knew, and we didn't.

When you start doing this, you start to become a Master Prospector!

Most importantly, you want to get everyone on your team to focus on getting customers, too. Happy customers are the life-blood to your Network Marketing organization. Don't ignore them!

Don't be afraid to try the methods taught in this chapter.

The idea of duplication begins here…

> Just imagine if you had everyone on your team mailing 100 family and friends every month!
>
> If you have just 10 team members that would be 10 x 100 = 1,000 exposures!
>
> If you have just 100 team members that would be 100 x 100 = 10,000 exposures.

Done correctly, you can reach some of the highest ranks in your program.

In the next Rule. we will be showing you how to build your business by using our Telephone Interviewed Leads.

I want to caution you for a moment before you read the next Rule.

Go ahead, right now, and make a list of 100 family, friends, co-workers and even previous business partners in other direct sales programs.

Get their physical address, not just their email.

The psychological power of a mailed letter is a tremendous recruiting tool for you.

When you mail a letter to someone you know, it then becomes real to them.

Why?

Because you wouldn't have bought the envelope, written a letter, printed it out, folded it into an envelope, address it and pay to put a stamp on it unless it was real!

Even if you have contacted them before about an opportunity, that doesn't mean that you shouldn't contact them again.

This is why the mailing a letter first and then calling them the next week and asking if they've watched your video and who you should talk to works so well.

It's about exposure, not about pre-judging.

Remember, most people have not improved their financial condition since the last time you spoke with them.

The key here is EXPOSING your 100-people knowing that the person you are really looking for isn't on that list of 100.

Instead, you'll find that person from a referral you ask for.

Your goal is to get a minimum of 100 referrals from your phone calls to your family and friends…try for more!

That's why we word it the way we do.

It's a take-away method in sales that works.

Try it, we think you'll be pleasantly surprised!

We know you can go to the top with this method alone!

But, if you or your team are not interested in contacting your family and friends here is another proven method that we use to contact other like-minded entrepreneurs called Telephone Interviewed Leads.

Here's a quick guide of who you know. Go to your phone:

Friends and Acquaintances

Your Best Friend	Your Other Friend(s)	Next Door Neighbor(s)
Other Neighbor(s)	Mom's friend(s)	Dad's Friend(s)
Son(s) Friend(s)	Daughter(s) Friend(s)	Your Boss
Favorite Co-worker	Other Co-Workers(s)	Your Boss's Boss
Twitter Friend(s)	Facebook Friend(s)	Instagram Friend(s)
Linked-in Friend(s)	Forum Friend(s)	Social Networking Friend(s)
Your YouTube Friend(s)	Your NWM Friend(s)	Your BNI Group
Grammar School Friends	High School Friends	College Friends
Chamber of Commerce	Toastmasters.org	Knights of Columbus
Fraternity Friends	Sorority Friends	Your Teacher(s)
Your Christmas Card List	Friends from Church	Spouse's Best Friend
Sent You Christmas Card	Sent You Birthday Card	Who Calls You At Home?

Social Contacts

Who do you play cards with?	Who do you play golf with?
Who do you play tennis with?	Who do you work out with?
Who do you go Bowling with?	Who do you go to concerts with?

Business Contacts

Who Sold You Your House? (Realtor)	Who Sold You Your House? (Old Owner)
Who Sold Your Old House? (Realtor)	Who Bought Your Old House?
Who Gave You a Mortgage?	Who Sold You Home Insurance?
Who Sold You Life Insurance?	Who Sold You Car Insurance?
Who Sold You Health Insurance?	Who Sold You An Annuity?
Who Sold You Your Car?	Who Sold Your Spouse a Car?

Who do you know in each state in the USA?

Who do you know in every foreign country?

Your Relatives

Your Mom	Your Dad
Your Sister(s)	Your Brother(s)
Your Niece(s)	Your Nephews(s)
Your Grandson(s)	Your Granddaughters(s)
Your Grandfather(s)	Your Grandmother(s)
Your Son(s)	Your Daughter(s)
Your Mom's Sister(s)	Your Mom's Brother(s)
Your Dad's Sister(s)	Your Dad's Brother(s)
Your Male Cousin(s)	Your Female Cousin(s)
Your Favorite Aunt	Your Favorite Uncle
Your Mother-In-Law	Your Father-In-Law
Your Sister-In-Law(s)	Your Brother-In-Law(s)

Robert Says:

In the beginning of my career I was afraid to talk to my family and friends. I was running a printing press for my Father for just $10 an hour. I felt I had no creditability to talk to anyone about making money. When I discovered I could also lead with our products I became very excited because I already had a couple of really good testimonials from my Mom and a few of her friends along with my own. When I started calling and mailing people a brochure and asked them *"who do you think I should talk to"*, over half said *"what about me?"*. That's when I really gained confidence in myself and this business.

Sheri Says:

Being a mom of 5, I've spent lots of time at the park, birthday parties, play dates, sporting events. You name it, I've been there. I have found that these are great places to engage in product conversations. With the kiddos on the products, parents would ask about them. *"Hey where did you guys get that?"* Nonchalantly I would explain that they came from our business, and oh by the way, you can order some too. Sometimes product curiosity can open windows. And a nice added touch was a sample I pulled out of my bag. Make it as natural as asking about a new movie. Love it or hate it, you don't try to sell them on going or not going to the movie. You inform them on what you liked or disliked about it. You leave it to them to decide whether to go or not to go. Ask for referrals. This a good way to build your confidence!

RULE #3: CONTACTING PEOPLE YOU DON'T KNOW

We didn't start our Network Marketing career by looking to contact people we didn't know. It just kind of happened over time.

We followed Rule #2 religiously. It worked for us, it worked for our team. But, not everyone on our team would mail their family and friends. In fact, if we forced the issue on them, they threatened to quit and drop out.

Which left us with a very important question for them:

"If you aren't going to talk to your family and friends about your business, who are you going to talk to?"

Since we owned a printing company, we had contacts with publishers and mailing lists.

We began renting mailing lists and testing letters and postcards for a few months with very little success.

Then one day, we came up with the idea of taking those mailing lists and having a phone room call the leads for us before we mailed them.

And, it worked!

Now, when a team member says they won't mail their family and friends, nor will someone in their group, we introduce them to our Telephone Interviewed Leads. These leads are just a great way to talk to other like-minded people!

Telephone Interviewed Leads are people who have opted into a website looking for more information on starting their own business and/or making money from home.

We then take those leads and send them to a call center. They will dial between 25 and 50 people to get one interviewed lead who says they want someone to contact them about making additional money from home.

What information do you get with these leads?

- First and Last Name
- Email address
- Telephone Number
- Agent they spoke with (very important)
- How much extra money would they like to make monthly?
- How much time can they spend each week on growing their business
- If you found the right business would you invest at least $100 to get started
- Gender
- Best time to call them

What kind of response should I expect?

Having called over 50,000 leads in our career here's our averages:

- 100 calls made
- 20 to 40 appointments set
- 10 to 20 people will show up to the appointment
- 5 to 10 people will become a customer or a distributor
- Commit to at least 90 days of calling as it takes that long to see results!

Your goal is to call each lead, verify their email, send them a video to watch about your Network Marketing Program and set a follow up time to answer any of their questions.

When you speak with them on the follow up your goal is to start with the following:

Ask them qualifying questions to get them to either become a Retail Customer or a Wholesale Distributor.

There are only three possible outcomes when you call to set an appointment:

1. Get a live caller
2. Get a voice mail
3. No answer or no voice mail set up yet

Sample Phone Script

Get your list of prospects that you have received from ProfitLeads.com and sort them by morning, afternoon and evening contact times.

We'll be basing these examples here on calling 100 Telephone Interviewed Leads a month. We recommend calling 25 leads at one time, or at least 5 leads per day.

Speaking to a Live Prospect on the Phone:

> *"Hi is this (prospects name)? This is (your name) calling you from (your town). The purpose of my call is you recently spoke with a gentleman from my office by the name of Max (phone room agent's name) about our business.*
>
> *I'm calling today to just verify your email address, so I can send you a video to watch to see if this is a fit or match for you. If I give you a website will you watch a short video that tells you how our program works? (Have them verify their email, or read it to them) Great, here's how the process works (prospects name).*
>
> *Watch the video and write down any questions you have. We have a proven game plan to increase your income in the next 90 days with our program! You don't need any previous experience nor a lot of money to get started…just a desire to earn more and get ahead!*
>
> *What's a good time tonight or tomorrow to call you back to answer your questions and tell you about our 90-day game plan? Great, be looking for an email that says: We Just Spoke on the Phone. See you at 9pm tonight!"*

Be sure to take good notes and have your planner out when you are making phone calls, so you don't over-book appointments. Remember, only about 50% of those who set an appointment with you show up to the appointment!

So, the more relaxed and upbeat you are and less salesy or pushy, the more people will show up to hear about your proven 90-day game plan!

You can hear Robert call 25 Telephone Interviewed Leads and set 10 appointments at our Profit Leads website. Just click on the "Leads" tab and look for the link under our video to listen now!

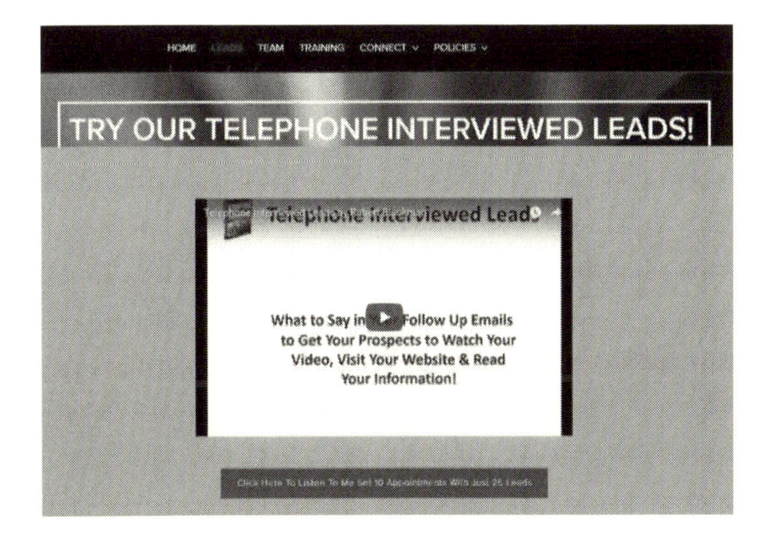

www.ProfitLeads.com

Email to Send to Your Prospect That You Just Spoke With on the Phone:

Subject, John, we just spoke on the phone

Hi John,

Here's the video I spoke to you about today:

www.YourWebsiteGoesHere.com

Watch the video, write down your questions and I'll call you at 9pm eastern time tonight per our conversation.

When I call you be sure you have a pen and paper as I'll be going over our proven game plan to help you make money in the next 90 days!

Sincerely,
Your Name
Your Phone

Leaving Your 1st Voice Mail:

"Hi John, this is (your name), and I'm calling you from (your state).

The reason for my call John is you recently spoke to a gentleman in my office by the name of Max about our business.

He took down your email at (read their email) and what I'm going to do is forward you a video to watch that explains more about how our program works.

We are looking for people in the Atlanta, GA area (mention their City and State) and I'd like to set up a time to talk with you about how we can significantly increase your income over the next 90 days with our proven game plan.

As you are probably aware, working from home is an exploding market, and we have a proven system where you can get involved with us for little or no money down!

Be looking for an email from me that says:

John, I just left you a voice mail.

Watch the video, write down your questions and either email or call me to set up a time to chat.

Enjoy the video and I look forward to going over our program with you, have a great day!"

(You can also text them per page 55)

Leaving Your 2nd Voice Mail:

"Hi John, this is (your name), and I'm calling you from (your state).

You had spoken to Max about our business and I sent you an email with our information to review.

He took down your email at (read their email) and what I'm going to do is forward you a video to watch that explains more about how our program works.

Give me a call back if you're looking to change your financial situation in the next 90 days.

Thanks!

(You can also text them per page 55)

Leaving Your 3rd Voice Mail:

"Hi John, this is (your name), from the XYZ company giving you a call again.

I know you showed some interest when you spoke with Max recently and I'm going to text you more information about how you can get started with us.

We are interviewing other candidates and will be choosing our team by this weekend.

Look for my text and if you're interested, just text or call me back…have a great day!

(You can also text them per page 55)

Email to Your Prospect That You Left a Voice Mail Message for:

Subject, John, I just left you a voice mail

I just left you a voice mail message.

Here's the video to watch:

www.YourWebsiteGoesHere.com

Watch the video, write down your questions and email me or call me to set up a time to go over how our program can increase your income over the next 90 days!

Talk to you soon.

Sincerely,

Your Name

Your Phone

PS Watch the video and email or call me to schedule a time to go over it. I have a proven 90-day game plan for you!

If you are going to contact the leads that you get from us each month use the emails and phone scripts to call, text and email them.

You can simply send them to your site and ask them to WATCH the Video.

There are many options for you to choose from when it comes to videos.

Our suggestion is to find a video you like and are excited about on your company's YouTube Channel or your very own website.

Do not send them to another landing page where they must opt-in again!

That's the kiss of death.

You want them to watch your video, read your .pdf or listen to a recorded phone call. That's the #1 Goal you have when you set an appointment.

Set the appointment, get the video to them, follow the closing questions listed in this training!

What you want is for your prospect to watch a video and then ask you questions. We suggest sending them to your replicated website if they want more information.

And, don't be afraid to take their order over the phone, or even 3-way them into your company. Do not, and I'll repeat, do not TRUST that they will go back to your website "later" and join. 99% of them will not and you'll lose them forever.

Take their order while the "iron is hot!" You can also, in most companies, just login to your back office and enroll a customer or distributor there.

Remember, if someone is "open" it doesn't matter what you get to them, a brochure, a VIDEO, a website, an interview, a conference call, etc. If they are NOT open, then nothing will work.

So, don't get caught up on trying to figure out which is the best tool to use.

I would email them at least once a week until they respond with a no or yes.

If you call one of the leads and they don't answer, or they don't have a voicemail that's been set up yet, send this email:

Email to Your Prospect With No Voice Mail:

Subject, John, I just tried to call you

Hi John,

I just tried to call you!

You spoke to Max from my office a few days ago.

He said you were researching ways to make money from home.

Here's a video to watch about our business:

www.YourWebsiteGoesHere.com

Watch the video, write down your questions and email me or call me to set up a time to go over how our program can increase your income over the next 90 days or less!

Talk to you soon.

Sincerely,

Your Name

Your Phone Number

PS Watch the video and email or call me to schedule a time to go over it. I have a proven 90-day game plan to get you making money, working part-time, from home with little or no previous experience necessary.

(You can also text them per page 55)

Important Texting Tip:

You can also text your video link (or website) to your prospects and remind them of the appointment time to increase your show up rates.

Texting is a very effective way to get your prospects attention and always remind them of the agent's name they spoke with at the phone room!

In fact, here are 30 MIND BLOWING FACTS about texting:

1. 97 percent of Americans use texting at least once a day on their cell phones. (Pew Internet)
2. Over six billion texts are sent in the United States each day. (Forrester)
3. More than 80 percent of American adults text which makes it the most common cell phone activity. (Pew Internet)
4. Email has a 20 percent open rate, while text messages have a 98 percent open rate. (Mobile Marketing Watch)
5. Text messaging has a 45 percent response rate, while email only has a 6 percent response rate. (Velocify)
6. 90 percent of all SMS texts are read in under 3 minutes. (Connect Mogul)
7. On average, text messages are read in under 5 seconds. (SlickText)
8. 75 percent of worldwide cell phones are text-enabled. (DuoCall Communications)

9. An average adult uses a total of 23 hours per week texting. (USA Today)

10. On average, Millennials exchange 67 text messages per day. (Business Insider)

11. Americans exchange on average 2X as many texts as calls. (Nielsen)

12. Only 43 percent of smartphone owners make calls, but over 70 percent of users text. (Connect Mogul)

13. 55 percent of heavy text-message users (more than 50 texts per day) prefer to receive a text than a phone call. (Pew Research Center)

14. On average, it takes a person 90 minutes to respond to an email, but it only takes 90 seconds for them to respond to a text message. (CTIA)

15. Women in America text 14 percent more than men. (Nielsen)

16. 79 percent of businesses believe that customers prefer SMS/text support. (ICMI)

17. 61 percent of call centers will offer SMS text support in 2016. (Dimension Data)

18. 80 percent of people use texting for business. (eWeek)

19. 1/5 of consumers are just as likely to prefer an SMS message from businesses to a phone call. (ICMI)

20. Preferred texting activities are to check order status (38 percent), schedule or change an appointment (32 percent) and make or confirm reservations (31 percent). (Harris)

21. More than 1/2 of consumers would be likely to text with a customer support agent. 52 percent would prefer texting with customer support over current methods. (eWeek)

22. More than 1/3 of business pros cannot go more than 10 minutes without responding to a text message. (eWeek)

23. SMS texting converts a $6-to-$10 phone call to a pennies-per-session chat. (Forrester & ContactBabel)

24. Prospects that are sent texts convert at a 40 percent higher rate than those not sent texts. (Velocify)

25. Over 65 percent of marketers report SMS texting as being very effective. (ExactTarget)

26. 70 percent of consumers appreciate getting text messages from healthcare providers. (Loyalty 360)

27. 75 percent of consumers would like to have special offers sent to them via texting. (Digital Marketing Magazine)

28. More than 80 percent of consumers prefer no more than 2 marketing text messages per month. (Digital Marketing Magazine)

29. 20 percent of financial services use SMS messages to add to their multi-channel capabilities. (Loyalty 360)

30. 72 percent of professionals prefer SMS to messaging apps. (eWeek)

Sample Text to Those You Left a Voicemail:

First Text:

"Hi John, I understand you spoke with Max in our office recently and you shared that you were researching different ways of making money from home. Our company is looking for leaders in your area. If I send you a video with all the details, will you watch it? If so, what's your email? Thanks, Your Name"

Second Text After They've Answered Yes:

"Here's the video that gives you an idea of our company and how you can make money with us: www.YourWebsiteGoesHere.com I've got a Proven Game Plan to get you in profit quickly with our system. Watch the video and then text me a good time to talk so I can explain how this program can help you."

Text to Confirm Your Appointment with Those You Spoke With:

Text:

"Hi John, it was great speaking with you today. Here's the video to watch before our appointment at 7pm central time tomorrow. I've also emailed it to: (insert their email). Watch the video, write down your questions. At our appointment I'll show you how our 90-Day Game Plan works and how much money you can make! Thanks, Your Name

You can also text your video to your prospects an hour before the appointment time to increase your show up rates.

You can also send your prospects to your weekly conference call or webinar.

And, if you get an incorrect phone number, we replace those leads free of charge.

To order leads now go to: www.ProfitLeads.com

Robert Says:

I made a commitment of calling and mailing at least 5 leads a day, Monday thru Friday, or 100 a month. I figured if I could just sign up one new person a month it would be worth it long term. Especially when I realized everyone I signed up from our leads program had a list of 100 to 400 family and friends and referrals. It's what I call going to your *"cold markets, warm market"*. I realized after a few years that I had exhausted my list of family and friends, but my leads on the other end of the phone hadn't! That's when I really got excited about calling leads! This concept alone has made us millions of dollars, so I know it works if you just stick with it.

Sheri Says:

Love love love calling leads! Yes, I know that sounds a bit strange, but I do. At first, I was a little gun shy. What if they say no? What if they hang up on me? What if they cuss me? So. What if they do? Next. What if they want more information? What if they say *"where have you been?! I've been looking for a business I can work from home and didn't know where to start!"* What if they want to sign up right now?! Wow! Crazy right? I've heard all kinds of things making calls. Oh, but that's part of the fun. I like to turn calling into a game. Robert and I will see who had the most no's or who had the most live calls or who had the most yes's or the most "more info please". Make it a game! Be Michael Jordan! Take your shots!! What's the worst thing that can happen? They say no. Hmm. Oh well. You got this. Next!

RULE #4: YOUR FOUR CORE BELIEFS

Joining your Network Marketing company is step one.

You may have joined because a friend or family member introduced a great product or service to you that you love.

You may have joined from an online ad or a social media site.

You might want to make a few extra bucks on the side, or even replace your income at work and become a full-time Network Marketing Professional.

Whatever your reason for joining here are the four core beliefs we have found that you'll need to stay in the Network Marketing Profession long term.

#1 - Belief in the Profession

The following contains the ranking for the 2017 *DSA* Global 100 (based on 2016 revenues), an annual list of the top revenue-generating direct selling companies in the world. The list is published in the June issue of *Direct Selling News*.

1.	Amway	$8.80 billion
2.	Avon	$5.70 billion
3.	Herbalife	$4.50 billion
4.	Vorwerk	$4.20 billion
5.	Mary Kay	$3.50 billion
6.	Infinitus	$3.41 billion
7.	Perfect	$3.06 billion
8.	Quanjian	$2.89 billion
9.	Natura	$2.26 billion
10.	Tupperware	$2.210 billion
11.	Nu Skin	$2.208 billion
12.	Primerica	$1.52 billion
13.	JoyMain	$1.49 billion
14.	Jeunesse	$1.41 billion
15.	Oriflame	$1.40 billion
16.	Ambit Energy ++	$1.20 billion

17. New Era	$1.16 billion
18. Telecom Plus	$1.12 billion
19. Belcorp	$1.09 billion
20. USANA	$1.01 billion
21. Pola	$1.004 billion
22. Young Living	$1.00 billion
23. SUN HOPE	$940 million
24. DXN	$927.0 million
25. WorldVentures	$926.6 million
26. Isagenix	$924.3 million
27. Yanbal	$924.0 million
28. Team Beachbody	$863 million
29. Market America	$798 million
30. A C N	$750 million
31. Stream	$735 million
32. Tiens/Tianshi	$695 million
33. It Works!	$686 million

34. Team National	$659 million
35. Yandi	$644 million
36. Miki	$597 million
37. AdvoCare	$586 million
38. Arbonne	$541 million
39. Plexus Worldwide	$532 million
40. Rolmex	$515 million
41. PM International	$460 million
42. Scentsy	$456 million
43. LegalShield	$450 million
44. Le-Vel	$449 million
45. Omnilife	$375.93 million
46. YOFOTO	$375.92 million
47. Fordays	$365 million
48. Faberlic	$356 million
49. Kang Ting	$348 million
50. Nature's Sunshine	$341 million

51. 4Life Research $328 million
52. AnRan $321 million
53. Naturally Plus $300 million
54. NHT Global $288 million
55. LR Health & Beauty Systems $286 million
56. Merro $283 million
57. Menard Cosmetics $267 million
58. Family Heritage Life $265 million
59. Viridian + $263 million
60. Pro-Health $257 million
61. Noevir $249 million
62. Hy Cite Enterprises $233 million
63. Resgreen $232 million
64. KK Assuran $229 million
65. Take Shape For Life $222.4 million
66. CUTCO $222.0 million
67. Southwestern Advantage $218 million

68. LifeVantage $207 million

69. Kangmei $206 million

70. Pure Romance $203 million

71. Alphay International $200 million

72. Princess House $195 million

73. Mannatech $180 million

74. Charle $173 million

75. BearCere' Ju $170 million

76. Youngevity $163 million

77. Seacret $161 million

78. Kasley Ju $154.4 million

79. Longrich $154.4 million

80. Giffarine Skyline Unity $154.0 million

81. Marketing Personal $153 million

82. ARIIX $151 million

83. World Global Network $146 million

84. Naris Cosmetics $144 million

85. FuXion Biotech	$135 million
86. New Image Group	$124 million
87. Ideality	$115 million
88. Golden Sun	$103 million
89. Zurvita	$100 million
90. Diana Co.	$98 million
91. Vestige Marketing	$97 million
92. Global Ventures Partners	$92.1 million
93. Koyo-Sha	$91.8 million
94. Total Life Changes	$88 million
95. Immunotec	$82.2 million
96. Jimon	$77 million
97. Nefful	$75 million
98. Captain Tortue	$71 million
99. Shinsei	$69.4 million
100.Vision Int. People Group	$69 million

+ **Note:** As of July 2016, Viridian was divested from Crius Energy and is now a privately held entity. The Viridian International Management figure represents full-year sales generated by Viridian, inclusive of sales generated while operating under the Crius Energy Family of Brands, and sales generated for all product partners post-transaction.

++ **Note:** An earlier version of the 2017 Global 100 list contained an incorrect revenue figure for Ambit. The company has certified that its net sales were $1.2 billion, ranking it No. 16 on the Global 100.

Note: The final 2017 Global 100 list will be published in our June 2017 issue of *Direct Selling News*. (We are not responsible for any errors or omissions on this list.)

This is a great list for a couple of reasons.

One, it helps solidify that there are real companies, with real people making real money.

Two, anyone in your circle of influence who may try to say that Network Marketing isn't a legitimate business model, you can show them this list.

Part of becoming a Network Marketing Professional is knowing the FACTS.

That sets you up as the "Network Marketing Expert" in their life…and is a great way to get customers and Referrals!

According to the DSA in 2016 a record 20.5 million people were involved in Direct Sales.

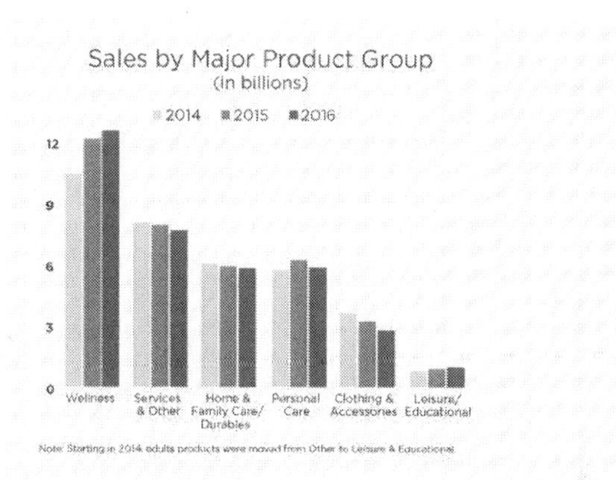

Over 5 million of these are building an independent business As direct sellers, meaning they are actively managing a customer base and possibly sponsoring others to do the same.

800,000 of these people are full-time and 4.5 million are part-time. In addition, 15.2 million others receive a discount on products and services that they personally enjoy and use.

Estimated direct retail sales of $35.54 billion in 2016 is the second most in direct selling history!

Yes, it helps if the company you pick is on this list, but it's not 100% necessary in order for you to be successful.

All this list does is show sales of those companies who have reported them to the DSA. Not everyone does.

Each of these companies were once a new start-up and they had to work hard to earn their way on it.

If you look and can't find your company on the list, don't despair.

Just know that you can be part of the reason they do get on the Top 100 list one day!

Use this list to help you build your BELIEF in the Profession.

#2 - Belief in Your Company

Get to know your company.

Know their "story" behind starting the company and behind Their products or services.

Then, tell their story.

Stories sell, facts tell!

If your company is debt free, tell that story.

If you're in several countries say so.

If they are 10 years old and solid make that a benefit.

Consequently, if they are brand-new, show your prospects what a great opportunity it is to be one of the first in your area to share the program with others before anyone else does.

- Dig deep into your company.
- Create a compelling story to tell.
- Visit the home office when possible.

- Go to your company conventions.

- Subscribe to all your companies Social Media outlets

Take pictures with the leaders and corporate staff for credibility and belief for you and everyone you share your program with.

Each company has a different "story" to tell.

Why they began in the first place. What's their company mission statement? What do they believe in?

Once you buy into their story, your confidence will grow. That makes it easier when a prospect doesn't show any interest in your program.

#3 - Belief in Your Product or Service

The reality is a very small percentage of the population:

- Have previous business or sales experience
- Have a high enough self-esteem to talk to anyone about anything

With that in mind, its vital that you and your entire team get their own product or service testimonial.

Why?

Because it may take a few months or even longer for you to get an income testimonial.

You don't want to find yourself saying:

"I'll talk to everyone I know once I make $1,000 in one month"

Don't fall into that trap.

Know that the majority of people you know won't be interested in the business right now.

They are too busy.

They might be financially challenged (don't prejudge!).

But, if you have a great product or service that can solve a problem, or one of their contacts have, then you have an opening to find a new customer.

And, happy, satisfied customers make the best distributors!

It's easier to find a customer than a distributor anyway. So, by leading with your product or service you will have a higher success rate.

In Rule #2 we talked about how to approach those people you already know.

We used the example of you owning a Yogurt Shop and approaching everyone you know to come on down and become a yogurt customer of yours.

Not all of your friends would want to buy a Yogurt Franchise like you did, but they'd be happy to buy yogurt from you.

This is the same attitude you should take towards your Network Marketing business.

This also allows you to contact your list of friends monthly with different specials on your products and services.

You and everyone on your team needs to have a personal

testimonial on as many of your products or services that you can!

#4 - Belief in Yourself

Zig Ziglar is famous for saying:

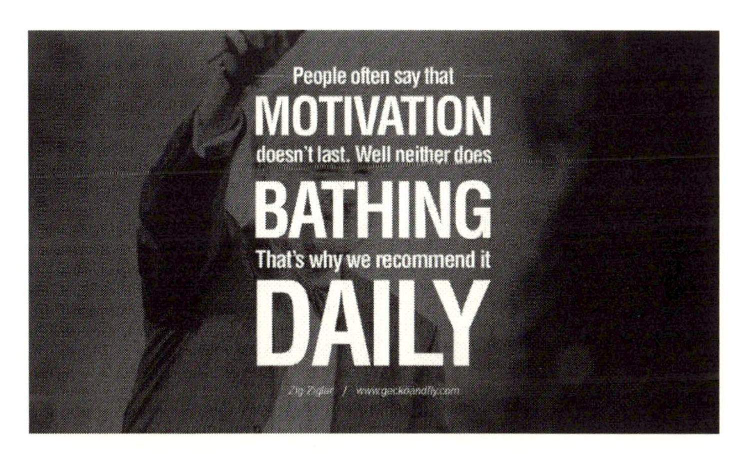

We find this is the most difficult belief for new people who join a Network Marketing program.

Why?

Because it takes daily consistent action.

You may look at a motivational book and say:

"I've already read that book, I don't need to read it again!"

But, how many times have you eaten at the same restaurant and ordered the exact same meal?

How many times have you watched one of your favorite moves and laughed out loud or cried as if you've watched it for the very first time?

Belief in one's self goes way beyond just being motivated.

You need to look at motivation as armor for your soul.

People are going to tell you no.

In fact, you'll get more no's than yes's over your career in this business.

People are going to tell you they are going to join with you or place an order, and they don't.

They say they will meet you for coffee and no-show you.

Both customers and distributors in your organization are going to quit ordering one day. Nobody orders forever, unless they are plugged into these four core beliefs.

1. Don't try to find the right person. Instead become the right person and you will attract them.

2. You can't say anything right to the wrong person, or if the timing for them is wrong.

3. You can't say anything wrong to the right person, or if the timing for them is right.

4. Every time you feed your body, feed your mind with books, CD's, videos, meetings, training calls, etc.

5. Plug into all the training provided by your company on their corporate website, your back office and all social media venues.

Robert Says:

For me I've always struggled with having all four core beliefs at one time. Then one day, a mentor of mine told me to look at each belief like a leg on a four-legged chair. If you just had one leg on the chair it would be impossible to sit on. Same goes with two legs. With three legs you could sit down, but you'd be wobbling around, and you'd get tired of trying to balance yourself. But, with four solid legs on the chair you'd have complete confidence when you sit down, as it is safe and secure. I've found that every six-figure income earner has all four beliefs in the Network Marketing Profession. They might not have started out with all four, but as their organization and their commission check grew, they eventually discovered all four on their own!

Sheri Says:

You must believe! I'm a believer. Are you? To find success in Network Marketing, you must have belief. Belief that this is a better way. Belief that the company you're with is THE BEST vehicle to get you where you need to be. Belief that their products/service will keep you coming back for more regardless of the pay plan. Belief that you've got this! That you are confident in yourself. You don't have to know everything, but you must have the will to try. To start. To believe that you can! Remember, your company will have training in place to help you become more confident, but you must give it a try. You don't have to be great to start, but you must start to be great! Thank you Zig Ziglar. You are absolutely right!

RULE #5: KNOW THY COMPENSATION PLAN

One of the most misunderstood parts of the Network Marking business model is knowing and understanding the compensation plan.

This rule will help you formulate a game plan for you and your team. One that duplicates, and gives everyone a layman's understanding of how you're going to get paid.

We estimate that over 95% of those that join a program don't understand how they get paid before they sign the dotted line.

Legally, you must be careful to make any guarantees or even projections without showing a disclaimer of what the average distributor in your company makes.

Always ask and look for that "Income Disclosure".

When reading it don't fall out of your chair.

Most Income Disclosure statements will show average earnings in the hundreds of dollars a month, not tens of thousands.

Why?

Because this is a volunteer army on 100% commission!

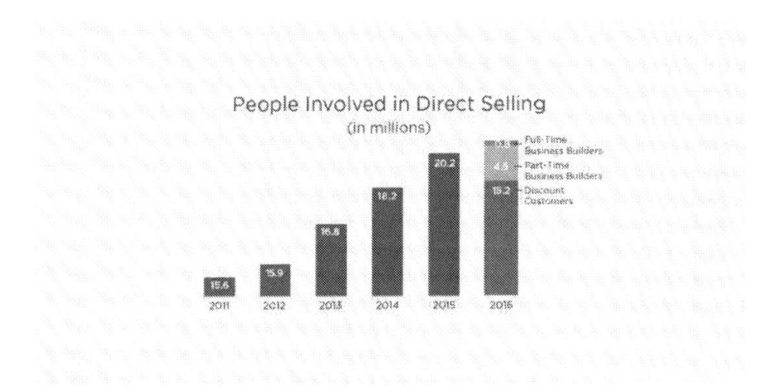

Look at the chart above provided by the DSA.

In 2016 there were 20.5 million people involved in Network Marketing (also known as Direct Selling).

- 15.2 million were just discount customers
- 4.5 million were part time business builders
- 800,000 were deemed full time business builders.
- 3.9% of all distributors are full-time
- 21.9% of all distributors are part-time

So, while looking at any Income Disclosure know that only approximately 25% of those that sign up do any recruiting activity to get customers or other distributors into the business.

This business model is about duplication, yes.

But, it's also about sales and team building. You'll need to learn and master both if you plan on not only quitting your job in 2-5 years, but making Network Marketing a permanent profession for you.

SALES will include earning retail commissions from customers or upfront bonuses on the purchases of first time distributors.

TEAM BUILDING will include developing an organization who does the same with both customers and distributors.

"Nothing happens until someone sells something" is the motto in Network Marketing!

Before we go into explaining the different types of compensation plans and how you get paid let's go over something that is vital to your Network Marketing business:

CUSTOMERS

Yes, customers.

Customers are the life-blood of any sales organization.

They are also necessary to make the Network Marketing business model legal in the eyes of the regulators.

We suggest you get a Customer Acquisition Program (C.A.P.) going for your business right from the start.

Most Network Marketing programs will have websites and brochures that help you retail your products.

Here's an example of a successful campaign we designed with a company who sold an anti-oxidant capsule for a 30-day supply that wholesales at $29.95 plus $5 s&h for a total of $34.95.

Once we visited with many of the top reps and customers we quickly realized that their own problem was market penetration. To do that, we came up with the idea of doing a 30-day trial.

We created a $7.95 thirty-day trial to help all our distributors penetrate their warm and cold markets.

Feel free to model this C.A.P program and see how you can fit it into your current program and product line:

Retail to Recruit Customer Acquisition Program

How to use the FREE 30-Day trial to help you get more customers and distributors into your Organization!

Four Steps to Success:

STEP ONE: Enroll your customers into our Free 30-Day Trial for $7.95 for a bottle of our product.

STEP TWO: Make a follow up call/text on Day 7.

STEP THREE: Make a follow up call/text on Day 14.

STEP FOUR: Make a follow up call/text on Day 28.

STEP ONE: Introduce the 30-Day FREE Trial program to everyone you know with a product brochure, a FREE Trial order form, or direct them to your website.

They will place an order for $7.95 shipping and handling for one bottle of our Supplement. The day the company ships their product their 30-day trial begins.

(If your company won't do this, you can create your own C.A.P. You can call us, and we'll be happy to help you do this).

STEP TWO: On the 7th day after their product has shipped call/text your customer and say the following:

> *"Hi (their name) this is (your name) calling from XYZ company. I just wanted to make sure you have received your free 30-day shipment of our supplement along with the DVD? (Wait for answer). Be sure you open the product, take 2 capsules a day and watch the DVD. Also, put the bottle in the refrigerator after you open it. And, in a week I'd like to follow up with you and see how you are doing. Sound good?"*

STEP THREE: On the 14th day after their product has shipped /text your customer and say the following:

> *"Hi (their name), this is (your name) calling from XYZ company. About a week ago I said I'd call you to follow up. How's it going? (Wait and listen for their answer). Now (their name), would you like for me to show you how to save on your next purchase with us? I'm sure you know of a few people who could benefit from our product by trying it for FREE for the next 30 days. I will be happy to mail up to 10 people a brochure about our amazing new product and the 30-day trial!"*

STEP FOUR: On the 28th day after their product has shipped call/text your customer and say the following:

> *"Hi (their name) this is (your name) calling from XYZ Company. I'm calling today to let you know that in a few days your next bottle is getting ready to ship. (1) Would you like for me to show you how to save money at wholesale, or would you like to pay the retail price instead? (2) And, out of those 10 names that you gave me, 5 of them have also taken the FREE 30-Day Trial, just like you did. My question is, would you*

like for me to get the commission, or would you like to make the money instead?"

(If they stay on as a preferred retail customer they pay $36.25 per bottle and you earn a retail bonus + 15% in overrides. If you upgrade them to a Distributor you earn a Fast-Start Bonus on their first month's purchase!)

OVERVIEW

The main purpose of the ***"Customer Acquisition Program"*** is to help you build your business by obtaining customers first.

You get them as a retail customer first. Then, you recruit them as a repeat customer or even as a distributor.

It is a proven fact that it is easier to get a customer than it is to get a distributor in the Network Marketing Profession, this C.A.P. helps you do that.

Another proven fact is a satisfied customer becomes a very excited distributor once they have a personal testimony of your product or service.

With that in mind, the 30-day trial is designed to make it easier for you to contact everyone you know with a brochure and a low-key approach:

"Try this for the next 30 days to see if it can help you!"

The customer pays $7.95 for shipping and handling to receive one bottle or a 30-day supply of your product.

On days 7, 14 and 28 you will need to make a follow up phone call to them with the suggested phone script.

Day 7 is not a long conversation. You are simply calling them to verify they have received their product, (If they haven't, help them contact the company to insure their order went through and to the correct address. If you're doing this on your own it makes it easy as you are the one taking the order and shipping the product). It is also a chance for you to remind them to take the product as described. This is very important. Unless they take the product, they won't re-order it. So, don't miss this first call. Most people's lives are very hectic today, and a friendly call to remind them will help improve your results tremendously! Also, encourage them to watch the DVD that is in their package. And, before you end the call, ask them if it is alright if you call them in a week to check in on them. This is building a relationship with the customer. It also sets them at ease that they made a wise decision by taking the 30-day trial. You'll also notice we told the customer to put the bottle in their refrigerator after they opened the bottle. Why? Not because it's perishable, but because the average American opens their fridge 15-20 times a day. Thus, reminding them multiple times a day to take the product!

Day 14 is a little longer conversation. Your purpose on this call is twofold. One, you want to ask them *"how's it going"* with the product. Some will be taking it every day while others will have not taken it at all. Out of every 10 customers one or two may cancel at this time. Don't let that discourage you. Nobody in business has a 100% success rate. Don't set yourself up for failure by thinking everyone who tries our product will stay on it for the rest of their lives! That just won't happen and isn't realistic. So know the numbers and expect some to drop out at this time.

For those that are taking it and seeing success immediately, go into getting a list of up to 10 referrals from them for you to meet, call, text, email or send a brochure to in the mail.

For those that are taking the product but are not seeing any immediate results encourage them to take the full 30-day supply before making any judgments. Just like a prescription from your doctor, you must take the entire dosage to insure results. You can also take this opportunity to tell your own personal testimony on the product. Or, share testimonies of those the company provides you.

Secondly, day 14 is important for you to get all referrals that you can from your customer. Some of the customers you will never be able to get hold of. Other customers you do get hold of on the phone won't give you any referrals at all. What is important about day 14 is that this is your second follow up in two weeks with them. Hopefully you are building rapport with them and they will feel comfortable giving you a few people to contact. Remember to let them know that YOU will be contacting their referrals with a mailed brochure/video for just the 30-day trial. Take this list over the phone or have them email you a list of names. Or, if you are in the same town, meet in person and take the names down then. Call their referrals for their street address by saying:

> *"Hi (their name) my name is (your name) and I was referred to you by (your customers name). I'm with a company by the name of XYZ. (Your customers name) is trying our product for free for the next 30 days and he/she recommended I contact you, so I could mail/text you some information about our product as well.*

At this point, don't answer too many questions or spend too much time on the phone. Just get the address, be polite and hang up.

Day 28 is where you can convert your customer into a distributor. Again, not everyone will convert. If you have 10 customers, be very happy if 2 or 3 turn into distributors. Most people have no previous sales or business experience. When it comes to joining a business, and making a commitment to perform, they will hesitate, or their lack of self-esteem will hold them back. That is why getting them on the product is so important. If you join a business to make money, and in 90 days, you are not making any money, you feel like a failure. But, if you join as a customer for a health issue, and in 90 days you feel better, you feel like a success! See the difference?

You have from day 14 to day 28 to convert any referrals you have received into customers on the free 30-day trial. Plus, if you do this program properly and you get at least 1 to 4 new customers a month, you will NEVER run out of people to talk to!

The Retail to Recruit program can provide you with an ENDLESS SUPPLY of prospects and customers.

How well can this program work?

Here's the results we had with a company that had just 700 active reps.

The management was a bit skeptical when we first introduced this idea to them. So, they didn't allow the following:

- No phone orders
- No internet orders
- Mailed or faxed orders only!

We both knew this project would work, and we were willing to do it out of our own garage, but the company didn't want us to do that.

They wanted to take the orders and ship the products, which we were happy that they decided to do. We ended up with almost 3,000 customers in just three months!

Here's three charts to show you proof how this program succeeded, even when you could only mail or fax your order in.

New Retail and Preferred Customers by Week:

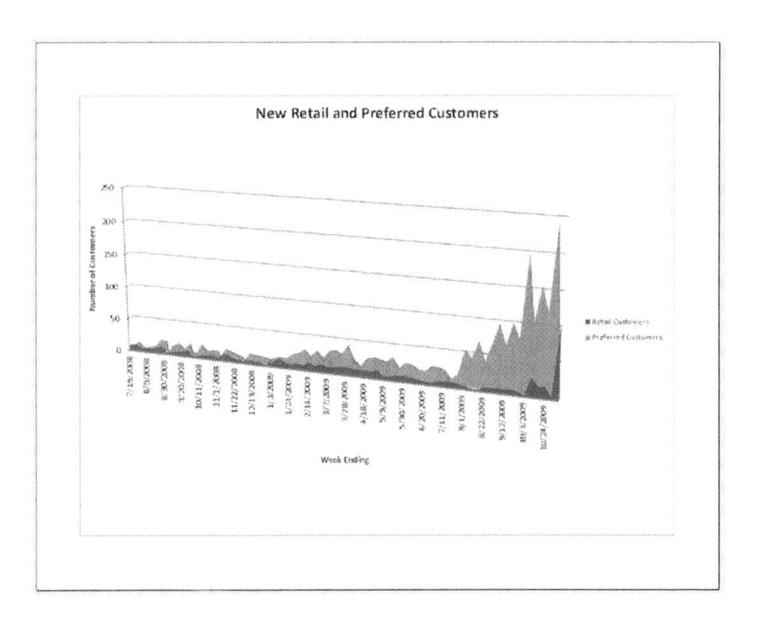

Free 30-Day Trial Customers by Week:

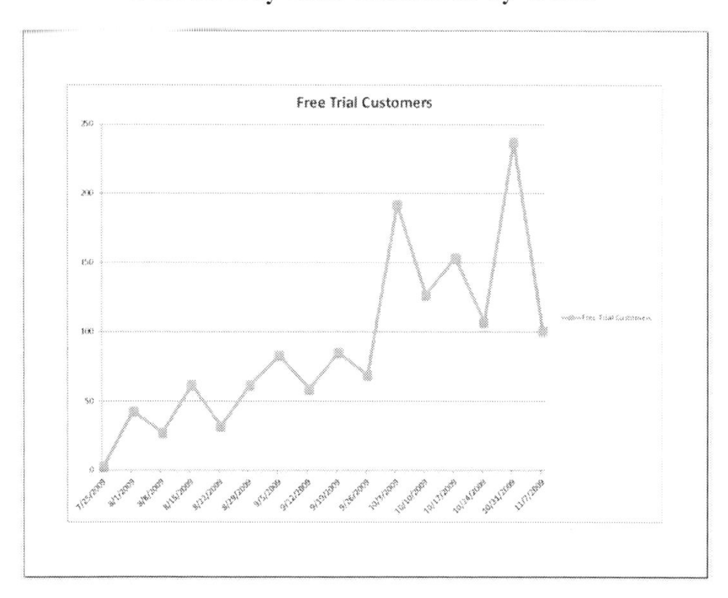

Total Customers of Almost 3,000 in three months!

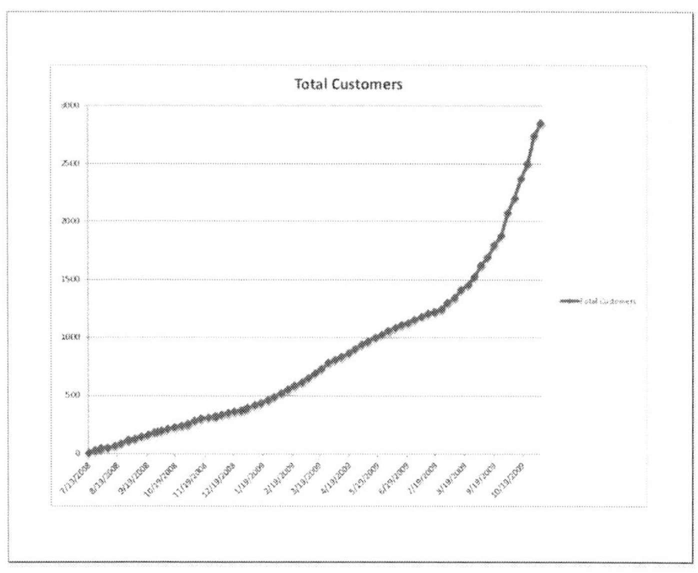

If your company doesn't have a C.A.P. in place, ask them to do so.

If they won't, contact us and we'll help you do one on your own.

You must have a product/service, of course, that works.

Ours showed results in less than a week, so we'd have people on our Day 7 and Day 14 calls asking for more product.

Or, giving us more people to talk to that needed the help the product was producing.

It created an excitement that we have seldom seen in our career. People's lives were being changed!

Distributors were gaining self-confidence because they felt comfortable talking about a $7.95 product that could help people they knew.

Customers were willing to spend $7.95 on a product they had never tried before from a trusted friend.

See how this works?

Therefore, you need to include a Customer Acquisition Program like this in your retailing game plan. It will put money in your pocket quickly and the pockets of your downline as well.

Now that we've spent some time going over how to retail your product or service with a C.A.P, here's what you need to know about compensation plans:

Our philosophy on sharing the compensation plan and how you make money in Network Marketing is very simple.

There are several types of compensation plans that you may be exposed to, such as:

- Uni-Level (unlimited first level, pays on levels and total volume in your organization)
- Binary (two legs, pays on volume not levels)
- Matrix (a fixed number of people on your first level, a fixed number on your second level, etc.)
- Stair-Step Break Away (like a uni-level with unlimited first level, but certain legs based on volume break away from your and you are paid a smaller percentage of their volume)
- Hybrid (combination of any above)

There are many books and articles that will articulate the pros and cons of each plan, which we will not be diving into here in our book.

Instead, we are going to teach you a formula or game plan to make a certain amount of money in ANY of the pay plans listed above.

First, know this.

The average commission you will earn is approximately 5% of your total sales. We know this can be larger or smaller based upon your compensation plan.

We also know that each compensation plan rewards you in more commissions as you move through the "RANKS" of the program.

But, for this illustrative purpose we are going to estimate a 5% commission overall volume.

Most companies will also pay on a percentage of the wholesale price, such as:

- BV (business volume)
- CV (commissionable volume)

For instance, you buy product as a distributor for a wholesale price of $100. The company may only pay commissions on the BV or the CV of say 80%.

- $100 wholesale
- $80 bv or cv

So, your commissions are paid on the bv or cv, not the wholesale price.

The company will also have rank advancements and/or qualifications for you to earn commissions on certain levels based upon:

- PV (personal volume)
- GV (group volume)
- QV (qualifying volume)

For example, let's say you just came in as a distributor. Your company has different ranks to advance through higher payouts in the compensation plan based upon sales volume in your group.

Depending upon your type of compensation plan, the math could be a bit different than our examples.

Let's have some fun and do the MATH on how much sales you need in order to make a particular income.

$300 Check
$6,000 in sales x 5% = $300 commission
30 people at $200 a month in sales
60 people at $100 a month in sales
120 people at $50 a month in sales

$500 Check
$10,000 in sales x 5% = $500 commission
50 people at $200 a month in sales
100 people at $100 a month in sales
200 people at $50 a month in sales

$1,000 Check
$20,000 in sales x 5% = $1,000 commission
100 people at $200 a month in sales
200 people at $100 a month in sales
400 people at $50 a month in sales

$2,500 Check
$50,000 in sales x 5% = $2,500 commission
250 people at $200 a month in sales
500 people at $100 a month in sales
1,000 people at $50 a month in sales

$5,000 Check
$100,000 in sales x 5% = $5,000 commission
500 people at $200 a month in sales
1,000 people at $100 a month in sales
2,000 people at $50 a month in sales

$10,000 Check
$200,000 in sales x 5% = $10,000 commission
1,000 people at $200 a month in sales
2,000 people at $100 a month in sales
4,000 people at $50 a month in sales

The number of people at each level are active people. As your organization gets older you will have more inactive than active people. This is normal, so expect it.

You must understand that this is why we teach a 2-5 year plan to replace your income at work…minimum.

It takes time, dedication, and duplication to be successful in Network Marketing.

Yes, there are always those stories of someone who just found the right person or two and then they sit back and collect a check and do nothing.

That happens, but we don't bet our bills, nor our retirement on that kind of thinking and neither should you!

Also, these are estimates based on an overall commission paid to you of 5% based on your monthly volume.

You may or may not qualify to earn commissions on all the volume under you, each month, unless you have met your companies pin levels to be paid on all your volume.

So, get with the company, your sponsor, or upline on what your qualifications are in your plan, so you're educated.

The examples on the previous page are your monthly residual commission check.

This does not include any upfront fast start, first order bonus or coding bonuses your company might have.

Nor, does it include any monthly bonus pools, car bonuses or leadership bonuses most plans have for top distributors.

So, when you look at your monthly income potential, know that you have three types of income:

#1 – Upfront bonuses on first month purchases
#2 – Monthly residual income on recurring purchases
#3 – Leadership or bonus pool for top reps

When we talk with a prospect or a new distributor we always go over how to break-even first.

So, if they join at $99 or $499 we show them how to quickly get that money back in their first 30 days.

We use the techniques in Rule #2 on mailing and calling at least 100 of their family and friends with the goal of getting at least an average of 3 referrals from each for a total of 300 additional contacts.

That's a database of 400 people to work with. Out of this list you can not only break even, but get into profit the first month.

Our goal is to always get our new recruits to at least the first Pin level in the compensation plan in their first 30 days.

The second pin level in their first 60 days.

And, the third pin level in their first 90 days.

We call that a "90-Day Blitz" or "90-Day Game Plan" to get someone to the third pin level or higher.

Let's say your first three pin levels are called:

- Bronze
- Silver
- Gold

Bronze is $1,000 in sales and three frontline customers or reps to achieve it.

Silver is $2,500 in sales and three frontline customers or reps to achieve it.

Gold is $5,000 in sales and three frontline customers or reps to achieve it.

You have two goals when you first get started, or over your next 90 days regardless of how long you've been in your program.

> #1 – Get to Bronze in 30 days. Silver in 60 Days.
> Gold in 90 days.
>
> #2 – Get your downline to do the same. (It's like shampooing your hair…just rinse & repeat!)
> With upfront bonuses you should be able to get yourself and your team to the following income levels in their first 90 days:
>
> > Bronze in 30 days = $300 in commissions
> > Silver in 60 days = $500 in commissions
> > Gold in 90 days = $1,000 in commissions
>
> Again, <u>these are estimates</u>, but you MUST find out how much you can make on your first three pin levels (or more) in your first 90 days!
>
> You won't believe how POWERFUL this concept is to not only getting yourself into profit, but to motivate and train your entire team to duplicate you.
>
> Done correctly, YOU can get to the top of your compensation plan in the next 12 to 36 months!

And, you can achieve that with understanding nothing more than the first three levels of the compensation plan and achieving them in the first 90 days!

This is key to this business, getting yourself and everyone on your team through the first few pin levels and a check in their hands!

You don't need to know everything about your compensation plan to get started.

But, you do need a 90-day financial game plan.

By doing this it creates a sense of URGENCY. A sense of urgency for you to get off your butt and make that list of 100! A sense of urgency to ask them for their physical address so you can mail them a letter like we explain in Rule #2!

It also helps you get your team off and running quickly. When you ask them for a list of names and addresses and they procrastinate you can say:

"Look, if you mail 25 letters a week for the next four weeks we will get you to Bronze or $300 in commissions, maybe even more. In fact, we have a proven game plan to get you to $1,000 a month in just 90 days. So, I need those names and we will also get a ton of referrals from those 100 names you give me, so let's go, go, go!"

Tell your team:

"I'm going on a 90-day blitz, are you in or are you out?"

Robert Says:

The first night I saw someone draw circles on a whiteboard I was hooked! I stayed up all night re-drawing their plan on sheets of paper all over the kitchen table. I had never seen such a business model where all I had to do was talk and point as many people as I could to someone else who would pick, pack and ship products to them and then pay me a commission! Coming from the printing, manufacturing business, I knew how much money and time it cost to keep a plant open, hire people, keep up with inventory, waste, returns, accounting, legal issues, etc. Network Marketing companies do ALL THE HEAVY LIFTING FOR YOU. Get out of their way and let them do it for you and just spend the rest of your life talking to and pointing people to them.

Sheri Says:

It's important to know how you're going to get paid. When you accepted your first job, I hope you accepted it knowing  how much you were to be paid. Everything we do we want to know the cost or how much we will be paid. It's how we budget our lives. Know thy compensation plan. How it works. Uni=level. Binary. Hybrid. Whatever it is. Get to know it. Your prospects will want to know. Compensation plans aren't easy for me. I'm a right brainer with a dash of left brain, but I study compensation plans. I want to know the many ways I can get paid through a compensation plan. Remember this is a business. And with this and any business, know how you will be compensated for your efforts.

RULE #6: CLOSING TIPS AND OVERCOMING OBJECTIONS

Okay, you've learned how to contact people. You've learned what to say to them.

Now, what happens if they ask you a question?

How do you maintain posture in this process and how do you guide them to signing up as a customer or a distributor, regardless of their questions or objections?

Closing tips: How to Close Your Prospects!

- It's a natural byproduct of following up with prospects at the appointment
- Exposure to Exposure is your job
- The goal is education & understanding your prospects
- You need good posture and command of the process
- You need to ask good questions, which puts you in charge

Here's how the Professional Network Marketer approaches "Closing"

-They are emotionally detached
-Their goal is education and understanding
-They are extremely assumptive and shocked that someone wouldn't want either the product/service/opportunity in their lives!
-Most amateurs are apologizing and don't realize it
-They know that people are joining with "them", and they take pride in that
-They are always prepared. Know your website, your pay plan, your cost of joining, products on hand, applications, the company number to 3-way them in. They know how to take an order in person and place it later, etc. Do This. Become a Pro!

After your prospect sees your information an Amateur says:

"What did you think?"

Professionals ask Leading Questions that invoke positive responses:

-Did it make sense to you?

-Pretty exciting, isn't it?

-What did you like best about what you saw?

-Who do you know who could use the product/service or the opportunity?

-On a scale of 1 to 10, 1 being no interest at all and 10 being you're ready to get started right away, where do you see yourself?

-Anything over a 1 is good!

Act like a Consultant, or a Coach and not as a Salesperson, to help them solve their problem.

Here's 4 Closing Questions Examples to Ask:

Question #1: "*Bob, based upon what you've just seen (or read or listened to), if you were to start with us on a part-time basis, about how much money a month would you need to earn, per month to make this business worth your time?*"

Then, just wait for the answer.

Never suggest a number like *"You'd like to make $10,000 a month, wouldn't you?"* Never say that. Now, it doesn't matter if they say $500, $1,000, $5,000 or even $10,000 a month.

Sometimes distributors fall into the trap of trying to sell a $10,000 a month opportunity and all your prospect really wants is an extra $500 a month. So, let them OWN their number, don't feed them a number, let them tell you what it is and that helps you identify who you are speaking with!

The key is to let them tell you what dollar amount is exciting to them!

Let's pretend they say $2,000 a month.

You say "great" and go to the next question.

Question #2: *"About how many hours a week do you think you could dedicate to this business to make that $2,000 a month?"*

Then, just wait for the answer.

Let's pretend they say *"10 hours a week"*.

You say "great" and go to the next question.

Question #3: *"About how many months would you be willing to work those 10 hours a week to develop a $2,000 a month passive, residual income?"*

Then, just wait for the answer.

You can get unreasonable answers here. They may want to make $10,000 a month and commit 2 hours a week and in 2 months' time.

Then as a consultant, with your *"consultant type mindset"* what do you need to do?

You've got to tell them that's an "unrealistic expectation". "But, if you're willing to change one of these 3 numbers, we can get you there". They must change the dollar amount, the number of hours and/or the number of months.

If they aren't willing to do that then say, this program might not be for you then.

Let's pretend they say "6 months"

Question #4: *"If I could show you how to get that $2,000 a month income, those 10 hours a week over the next 6 months, is there anything else you need to get started? Anything else you need to know to get started?"*

Then, just listen for the answer.

About 90% of the time they will say:

"If you can make that happen, then I'm ready to get started!"

By asking these questions and in this order, you've allowed THEM to create this reality that they can get excited about!

Some people are going to shock you and you'll think that they'll want $10,000 or more a month but all they really want is an extra $500 a month.

Maybe they've just had a talk with their spouse and they want to buy a new car, or fix up the kitchen, or they just want to pay off their credit cards!

Your job will be to help them create a "ROADMAP" in order to make that happen.

SUGGESTION:

I find that if you can help them reach their first or even second pin level in their first 90 days they will stay long term.

And, be sure to ***"Show Them the Money"*** when they get to those ranks!

We have built our career on calling leads.

We had to, as we ran out of people to talk to.

Trust this 90-day process.

Fill your pipeline with good prospects.

Don't get discouraged that someone doesn't join the day you

follow up with them. That rarely happens.

Just think of how long it took you to join after you heard about your opportunity.

Was it a day? A week? A month?

We call between 25 and 100 people a day with these techniques.

We never have to worry about having people to talk to about our program.

It is a great feeling knowing when you wake up in the morning not only do you have plenty of appointments, but that your entire organization does to!

Test our leads system now:

www.ProfitLeads.com

5 Ways to Overcome the Objection:

"Let Me Think About It"

What would telephone selling be like without a daily dose of:

"Let me think about it?"

Probably much easier and much less frustrating. But since the objection is not going to go away any time soon perhaps now is a good time to look at some ways to tackle it.

Is it Real?

When a prospect says, **"let me think about it",** is he telling the truth? Some prospects toss out this classic objection because they simply want to get rid of you.

They say it, not because they mean it, but because it is a polite method of getting you off the line. The trouble is, if you are not savvy to this brush off, you can waste a lot of time and energy following up with e-mails and phone calls.

On the other hand, some prospects really DO need time to think about it. Some need time to ponder their options, while others like to simply digest the information to ensure that they do not make a snap decision.

The challenge here is that if you are a cynical sales rep who has heard the objection time and time again, you may not take the prospect seriously and fail to follow up and hence, lose the opportunity.

So how do you tackle this devilish objection? Here are five ways to deal with this objection:

#1: Say Nothing

Here's how it works: when they tell you, they want to think about it, say nothing.

That's all there is to it. Just wait patiently.

Silence over the telephone creates a vacuum and most prospects get uncomfortable with the silence. After two or three seconds, most feel the compelling need to fill the void with words.

You will be absolutely amazed at how well this technique works if you can discipline yourself to hold your tongue for a few seconds. Typically, the prospect will elaborate on the *"let me think about it"* objection and this often uncovers the real objection.

For example, they might explain that they must speak to their spouse or their partner. Suddenly you discover another player in the game. They may reveal that they are looking at other proposals and now you know you are in a competitive situation.

Or they may simply not be interested at all. In any event, you have more information upon which to base your next step.

#2: I am Not Sure I Understand

This is a powerful response to the objection. When the prospect explains that they would like to 'think about it' pause for a second or so and then slowly say, *"I am not sure I understand."* The trick here is delivery.

Be subtle and use the tone of your voice to show surprised confusion, not belligerence. Do not utter a word. Let silence do its work. When the prospects hear the confusion in your tone they almost automatically feel the compelling need to 'come to your rescue' and elaborate further on their hesitancy.

#3: Give Them the Time and Get a Commitment

Another approach is to grant them the time but put a time limit on their pondering.

For example, Prospect: *"Well, let me think about it."*

You: *"I understand completely, John. A decision like this needs some time. And what I would like to recommend is that I give you a call next week to get your thoughts and to determine the next steps. How does Wednesday at 8:45 look on your calendar?"*

If the prospect accepts the recommendation the objection is probably legitimate. The prospect needs time for whatever reason. You know this because they have agreed to a specific time and date. It shows commitment.

Again, the key is to not only get a follow up date but also a specific time.

This approach is very non-threatening and is perfect for prospects who legitimately want more time. They will appreciate your courtesy and understanding. Therefore, you deliberately empathize with the prospect by saying you "understand."

These types of prospects do not like being cajoled or pressured. If you push too hard, they will say no to your offer because they do not like you and your 'aggressive' approach. Your offer could be extremely valuable and well-priced but these prospects value trust and relationship more.

If the prospect balks at your first suggestion, try another date and time and see if they positively respond. If they balk again, ask when would be a good time and date. If they cannot make a commitment, chances are they are brushing you off and your time is probably better spent elsewhere.

#4: Probe for Legitimacy

Here are some techniques to determine the legitimacy of the objection. Begin by empathizing with the prospect and then gently ask a question to get the prospect to clarify.

For example: Prospect: *"Let me think about it."*

Rep: *"I understand completely. If I were sitting where you are now, I'd probably want to think about it too. If I may, one quick question:"*

"what concerns do you still have? Or…

"what' is causing you to hesitate?" Or…

"what is your number one concern about not proceeding further?" Or…

"what will your final decision be based on?"

This type of probing gets the prospect to open and to help you determine if the objection is real or otherwise.

#5 The Level With Me Response

One of the best ways to deal with this objection is to ask the prospect to be completely candid with you. Here is how it works:

Prospect: *"I'd like to think about it."*

Rep, *"Fair enough. But John, we've spent a bit of time reviewing your situation and it looks like a good fit. Please level with me, what's holding you back?"*

The technique has a few things going for it. Note the use of the prospects name. It is used deliberately to create a bond of familiarity. It also gets the prospect to listen more closely. Next, the rep points out that a "bit of time" was used up and the implication is that the rep is at least owed an explanation. In addition, the rep uses a colloquial expression – level with me which in effect, is saying to the prospect 'hey, no games here, let's be honest with one another.'

Finally, there is the use of good old-fashioned politeness when the rep uses the word 'please.' It is a wonderful approach.

Summary

Don't let your prospect off the hook when you hear this objection. Try one of these five techniques and see how they work for you!

Robert Says:

I don't consider myself a salesman, even though that's really kind of what I do on a daily basis. I don't like being sold something and neither does anyone else. I consider myself a teacher, an educator of our products, services and profession. There are so many people who would love to quit their job and work from home but they don't know how to do it. They don't have a "back up game plan" like Sheri and I did. It took us four years to make our first $1,000 commission check because we did NONE of these 7 Rules when we first began our business. Follow the process we've outlined here. Know that not everyone is going to be as excited as you are about your business or products. It's your job to keep in touch with them and be a professional. And, when you do people will be attracted to you. People will reach back out to you and ask if "you're still in that thing", and want to meet with you!

Sheri Says:

We are all sellers in some way or another. Someone compliments your top, *"Oh thank you! I just got it at XYZ. Super soft! You would love it!"* They may ask you about a restaurant or plumber or vacation. Yep. Your recommendations sell. Those are nice and easy. When it comes to your business, it feels different. Maybe it's a bigger investment. Maybe they are unsure of your products. As you've heard many times, *The best defense is a good offense.* Get educated! Know your company in and out. The compensation plan. The products. Conference call and webinar schedules. Regionals and conventions. Everything you can! And get excited! Excitement is contagious. The knowledge and excitement you gain will help with the doubt and objections. "Hey guys we are super excited about our new business. It's taking off like a rocket! We would love to have you grow with us. Are you in or out?"

RULE #7: YOUR FIRST (OR NEXT) 90 DAYS

Now that you know what to do and what to say, here's a checklist to get you started over the next 90 days.

If you're brand new to Network Marketing then you can call this ***"Your First 90 Days".***

If you've been in a while and not really done a lot, or you had a group going but it fell apart, you can call this "Your Next 90 Days"

Here's Your Checklist for the Next 90 Days:

#1 Commit to mailing at least 25 letters a week for the next four weeks to people you already know. Text, email or call them to get their mailing address saying you're updating your contacts.

Mail 25 letters every Friday. Call those 25 the next week with the scripts in Rule #2.

Commit to at least calling five a day to see if they received your letter. Get the list of who they think you should talk to about your product/service/opportunity.

Use our sample letter and postcard in Rule #2. You have our permission to copy it directly or play off ours to make your own.

#2 Design and mail a postcard every month to your list of 100 personals and all the referrals they have given you.

If your budget doesn't allow it, mail a postcard quarterly, or four times a year. But, mail a postcard. It has very little competition in your prospects mail box. They have to read it before they throw it away.

Please put your picture on that card! Let them know it's you and here's what you're doing. Follow the sample we show you in Rule #2. Remember the Yogurt Shop example. If you owned one, you'd be mailing, emailing, calling and creating your own Facebook Fan Page to get customers.

Get customers. Be excited about your product or service. If you aren't excited, why will your potential customers be?

#3 Get a 90-Day Game Plan to reach at least your first pin level, but your goal is to get to your third one.

-Get to your first in 30 days.
-Your Second in 60 days.
-Your third in 90 days.

Show your team how much commissions are available at the first, second and third pin levels. Give them a target.

The amount of money you can make in your first few pin levels isn't going to be a million dollars.

It's going to be a few hundred.

Your goal is to get everyone mailing, calling, following up, setting appointments and signing up customers and distributors.

And, most importantly, get your members a check in their first 30 days!

You will be amazed at how much belief your team gains with a simple $25 or $50 check!

If you contact 100 people your first 30 days you are more likely to at least reach your first pin level in 30 days. So, don't string it out for months.

Have a sense of urgency and be disciplined and organized about it. When you sign up a new person, show them the money they will make and get them going ASAP mailing 25 letters a week for the next four weeks.

This is called duplication.

And, it's the simplest and purest form by mailing letters.

Left alone, most of your team will not call 25 people a week for a month. They may tell you they will do it, but it rarely happens.

That's why mailing a letter works. Everyone can do it with your help.

If you upline doesn't have such a plan take an evening or a weekend and go create it.

Put it in a .pdf and make it a tool that you give to all your downline members.

#4 The most important phrase you can say to your family and friends once they've watched your video or visited your website is this:

"Who do you think I should talk to?"

You are not asking them directly to join. You are asking them for a favor to watch something and then asking for a referral.

Again, what if you owned a Yogurt shop? You'd be networking yourself to death to make sales, wouldn't you ?

<u>Own that phrase.</u>

The likelihood of those you know being the one you are looking for are slim.

You want to turn your list of 100 into a list of 400 by getting 300 referrals from your 100. That's just 3 people each on average. Some will give you their entire rolodex or phone contacts if you have a product or service that really works!

#5 Mail the letters and do the follow-up calls every week.

-First week mail 25 letters.
- Second week, mail another 25 letters and call the 25 from week one.
-Third week, mailing another 25 letters and call the 25 from week two.
-Fourth week, mail another 25 letters and call the 25 from week three.
-Fifth week, clean up any bounced addresses and also mail any referrals you've had from your first few. Get your downline to duplicate this same five week process and your calendar will be booked solid with appointments!

Once you start sponsoring people, you'll want to insure they follow these rules. We suggest you call the first 25 letters they mail with them or even for them to show them how simple and easy it is to call and get referrals, and just follow the system.

Remember, your goal is to get to your first Pin level in 30 days. Your next goal is to help your downline to the same thing. Then, to help their downline do the same and so on. That's duplication in this business. Not everyone is going to do this. Don't push them. Just invite them to contact you once they are ready to get it going. Then, move on to those that are wanting to work with you now.

#6 Have at least two conference calls, zoom calls or webinars a week. We do our opportunity calls every Monday and our training calls every Saturday. If you don't feel comfortable doing them plug your team into ones your company or your upline does.

#7 Get some Telephone Interviewed Leads.

Starting at just $19.95 a month, it won't break the bank.

What it will do is get you and your team a consistent flow of hot prospects to talk to.

This especially works for those on your team who refuse to contact their family and friends. You will have them on your team, so expect it. Use this as an affordable alternative to build their business.

You have to show your group HOW they make money.

If not they get discouraged and quit.

Imagine a financial planner that never showed you a statement of your earnings?

Imagine a job where you didn't know how much you were getting paid until your check showed and then you'd say:

"This isn't what I thought I was getting paid!"

You and your team should know what your financial goals are and you should know specifically how many people and how much sales volume that is, regardless of what type of pay plan you're in!

#8 Now that you've shown your group how much money they can make with your program, go a step further--show them the MATH!

Yes, we like everyone on our team to have a PLAYBOOK and we like them to know how the plays are run!

It's not up to you to get them to study the Playbook and you can't make them run the plays.

But, as their "COACH" it is your job to show them the plays. Show them how to run and motivate them to *"strap on their gear"* and BUST SOME HEADS!

#9 I then make SURE <u>everyone</u> understands how much money they can approximately make at each pin level based on a certain amount of sales.

And, like a preacher who only knows <u>one sermon</u>, become comfortable teaching this to your team over and over again. Remember the chart from Rule #5 – Know Thy Compensation Plan:

$300 Check
$6,000 in sales x 5% = $300 commission
30 people at $200 a month in sales
60 people at $100 a month in sales
120 people at $50 a month in sales

$500 Check
$10,000 in sales x 5% = $500 commission
50 people at $200 a month in sales
100 people at $100 a month in sales
200 people at $50 a month in sales

$1,000 Check
$20,000 in sales x 5% = $1,000 commission
100 people at $200 a month in sales
200 people at $100 a month in sales
400 people at $50 a month in sales

$2,500 Check
$50,000 in sales x 5% = $2,500 commission
250 people at $200 a month in sales
500 people at $100 a month in sales
1,000 people at $50 a month in sales

$5,000 Check
$100,000 in sales x 5% = $5,000 commission
500 people at $200 a month in sales
1,000 people at $100 a month in sales
2,000 people at $50 a month in sales

$10,000 Check
$200,000 in sales x 5% = $10,000 commission
1,000 people at $200 a month in sales
2,000 people at $100 a month in sales
4,000 people at $50 a month in sales

Create something similar with a disclaimer, of course, that there is no guarantee of income, but these are projections and targets they can strive for!

That's our simple 9-Point SPECIFIC Goals for your next 90 days in the business.

It's basically EXPLODED our business! We've been able to "break down" how you and everyone in your downline gets paid!

Why is that important?

Because your downline has been trained to get paid so much an hour, or week, or month.

They do the work and they get a paycheck.

In Network Marketing, you join and you don't know how much you're going to make.

In Network Marketing you do the work at first and you may not see a check your first week or even first month.

Most drop out because they're used to getting paid for work done. When they don't get paid in this business model they feel something is wrong and quit.

It's your job to educate them on the process and simply walk them through your compensation plan.

Remember, if Diamond is the top pin level in your company and Bronze is your first pin level, you get to the top of your companies pay plan by "Building Bronzes"!

Yes, it's really that simple!

By building Bronzes day and night and having your team building Bronzes day and night, you will eventually find yourself at the top of the your pay plan at Diamond.

You'll be asked to speak at your next convention about how you got to the top, and all you'll have to say is:

"We just built Bronzes day and night for a couple of years and here we are standing in front of you not really knowing how it all happened so fast!"

Some people on your team will never engage in this process. Don't let it discourage you.

Go sponsor more new people with the people that you know, or the people that you don't know as outlined in Rule #2 and Rule #3.

Some people choose to buy a ticket and sit in the stands.

Some people choose to suit up for the game and ride the bench.

Some people even choose to suit up, enter the game and go through the "motions".

While others, like you, choose to play the game a bit differently. We both know that the more we help others, the more we help ourselves.

Go out today and set some specific goals that you and your downline can understand and achieve!

One of the most important things for you to do is set the following with your spouse/significant other or if you're single, with yourself:

Step 1: Set a monthly budget!

A. Set the days or nights of the week that you'll actually be working your business.

B. Set aside time to read at least one new book a month or listen to one CD/Audio/Video a month.

C. Always, and I mean always, plug into a weekly meeting in person or via the Internet. That could be a home meeting, a hotel meeting, a webinar or a conference call.

Step 2: Be sure to fill out your "Reasons Why" form and put it in your wallet, purse and stick it on your bathroom door and window.

Put it where you can see it at least once a day to remind you why you're adding this business model into your life.

People go back to college and get another degree or Masters all the time as an adult. They have to dedicate a couple days a week and several hours a day, along with a huge financial investment, to reach that goal.

Do the same for your business. Set the days you're going to work your business. Set your budget you're going to spend each month. Set an income goal after each 12 month period.

Remember, you are writing your own Social Security check, so don't give up on YOU!

Step 3: Create a similar version of the Goal & Commitment form for you and your group to use. This is a sample one from our primary program.

Feel free to edit and change it to fit your team goals. By having everyone on your team fill this out you get a clue who is willing to go to work *"now"*, not *"later"*. If someone doesn't fill it out after a month, you kind of have an idea where their commitment is, don't you?

Remember, you're not anyone's boss; you are their cheerleader and form of inspiration. Sometimes when someone joins that's the last form of action they'll ever take with you and your program. Don't fret. Give them a call and tell them you'd like a product testimonial from them. Get them hooked on the products. Like the TV jingle:

"I am stuck on Band Aid and Band Aids stuck on me!"

Do the same with your business. You want your products to *"stick"* to them, even though they aren't taking any daily action to build theri program.

Goal & Commitment Form

Name ______________________________Date_________

Address (City, State, Zip) ____________________________

Phone___________________E-mail_________________

Sponsor's Name_____________Phone__________________

I am on Auto-Ship each month for _____________ .

Total Monthly Advertising Budget____________________

Why I joined:____________________________________

My Greatest Strength is:___________________________

My Greatest Weakness is:__________________________

Check needed to quit work and go full-time:______________

30-Day Goal of XYZ Pin Level: _____________________

60-Day Goal of XYZ Pin Level: _____________________

90-Day Goal of XYZ Pin Level: _____________________

☐ I have mailed your 100 letters to your list of 100 family and friends

☐ You have ordered and called, emailed and text at least 100 Telephone Interviewed Leads

Signature_____________________________

The Philosophy Behind the "Goal" System

Accountability. Having everyone on your team fill this form out and fax it back is VITAL to your success. If you have 10 people in your group and only 5 fill it out and send it back to you, then you know who your "FIVE" are. These people are ready to work the business NOW, not later. You make money when YOU and your TEAM take action NOW, not next month or next year.

Budget. It's important for you and everyone on your team to know their budget and actually write it down on paper and share it with someone. Even if your budget is just $100 a month, don't be embarrassed. When I started this business I had to cancel my cable bill and change my spending habits just to come up with an extra $100 a month. So, you have to START somewhere. And, by writing down what your monthly budget is, you get to SEE it. Then you are personally committing to that and you will ensure that you save that much money a month for leads, postage, printing and training.

Goals. We've all heard of them and know we need them, but we hesitate when doing them. Why? After 56 years in this business, we believe most people are afraid to write down a goal. Usually they have low self-esteem and don't believe they can achieve their hopes and dreams. Plus, they don't want to write down a goal and share it with anyone, as it will then make them ACCOUNTABLE to someone else. Everyone knows that, for the most part, they are not taking daily action with their business. Because if they were, they would sign up more people and their check would be bigger.

Action. <u>Massive</u>, <u>consistent</u> <u>action</u> is the key. If everyone on your team just signed up 1 person out of 100 leads a month in 12 months your team would 2,048 members. But, that never happens, does it? Why not? Because not everyone takes action. That's why saturation never occurs. People fail to take action. This is why attrition occurs and why groups never get off the ground. If you focus on YOU first, then your downline next, you will succeed. Stop waiting for something to happen with your group. Focus on your own attitude and actions and your own written goals. Then and only then, will you start to see results.

System. The only way we know for you to generate a monthly residual income, that will keep coming in month after month, is for you to work a system. This system is the same one we've used in our primary programs to build Million Dollar Downlines. It starts with a simple concept:

"Go here and watch this video and tell me who I should talk to".

Then, get on at least 100 Telephone Interviewed Leads a month and contact 25 of them every week.

Tools. Know your website. Go to your companies website and read it. Print it out. Print out your Compensation Plan and put it on your desk. Know the commission schedule. Read all articles that are emailed to you. Get on the conference calls. Listen to your monthly training conference calls. Understand that if you're not doing the business, neither will your downline. Re-invest your monthly check into mailing letters, post cards, postage and leads. Yes, it's a numbers game…the more you contact, the more potential sign-ups you'll have!

Most people fantasize about becoming a success in this business, and that's all it truly is -- a fantasy.

How do you Become a Network Marketing Success?

As one top earner said,

> *The difference in me and others is that my vision for becoming a millionaire was crystal clear. I didn't drive it, IT DROVE ME. It was a fanatical urging that wouldn't go away.*

He said that vision became a PASSION in his life. That's a clue to what it takes to become a big success in Network Marketing. He added...

> *If most people would get as excited about their Network Marketing business as they do about a football game, they'd be rich within three years!*

Most people have the perception that Network Marketing millionaires are lucky. They found people who did all the work. Not so. Millionaires understand the TRUE numbers it takes to create massive success. Most folks are fantasy-based thinkers...that they can make 20 phone calls and get rich!

Another top earner gave this rundown of how she did it...

> *I knew all I had to do was talk to 1,000 people. That's what I was told to do and I was on a mission to do that. Instead I talked with over 3,000.*
>
> *Now I do what I want, when I want, for how long I want WITH MY KIDS! And THAT'S a miracle.*

Over 1,400 distributors were interviewed and here's the results:

Hours worked each week
Average: 6
Successful: 12
Millionaire: 25

Phone dials per day
Average: 5
Successful: 15
Millionaire: 50

People talked to per day
Average: 1
Successful: 7
Millionaire: 15

Presentations per week (phone or face-to-face)
Average: 2
Successful: 8
Millionaire: 20

Follow-ups per day
Average: 1
Successful: 4
Millionaire: 10

Number of no's per week
Average: 2
Successful: 10
Millionaire: 25

Number of new reps each week
Average: 0
Successful: 1
Millionaire: 4

Robert Says:

FAITH

Faith is when people tell you you're a fool and you can't possibly make it. They tell you if you had started when your company opened years ago you could have done it, but there's no way you can make it now.

The faith to keep dreaming when people are telling you:

"Hey, don't you know that it's a rip off?"

The faith to keep on going when people tell you no and reject you. Or people tell you yes, I'll show up and they disappear forever. The faith to get up the next morning when you've made some goals and plans that this is what I'm going to do by a certain date and it doesn't happen. To have the faith to get up and start all over again in spite of that. That is the faith we must demonstrate!

Sheri Says:

Alright! Alright! Alright! This is it! It's time to fly! Excitement is revving. Checklist in hand and Goal & Commitment Form filled. You've prepared yourself for this. With your preparation, your confidence is brimming. These 90 days will be amazing! Have faith in your abilities and stay focused. Use the tools you have with your company and the ones you have here in this book. Remember, it's not always going to be cupcakes and rainbows. You have a plan. Stick with it. If you fall into a lull, reach out to your upline, your company, to us! You are not alone on your journey. Network Marketing isn't just about networking to sell, it's also about networking to find like-minded people, whether they are in your company or not. It's a community. So, have faith. Enjoy the journey. And know, you got this!

RESOURCES

Telephone Interviewed Leads, Training & Coaching:

www.ProfitLeads.com

HOW TO CONTACT ROBERT & SHERI

Call us below:

Robert: (405) 833-6899
Sheri (405) 833-9899

90573097R00095

Made in the USA
Columbia, SC
06 March 2018